NISSAN
300ZX

NISSAN 300ZX

THE ENTHUSIAST'S COMPANION

RAY HUTTON

MRP

MOTOR RACING PUBLICATIONS LIMITED
Unit 6, The Pilton Estate, 46 Pitlake, Croydon CR0 3RY, England

First published 1990

Copyright © 1990 Ray Hutton & Motor Racing Publications Ltd

All rights reserved. No part of this publication may be reproduced, stored in a retrieval system, or transmitted, in any form or by any means, electronic, mechanical, photocopying, recording or otherwise, without the prior permission of Motor Racing Publications Ltd

British Library Cataloguing in Publication Data
Hutton, Ray
　Nissan 300 Z. X.
　1. Japanese cars, history
　I. Title
　629.22220952

ISBN 0-947981-52-7

Photoset in Great Britain by
Ryburn Typesetting Ltd, Halifax, West Yorkshire

Printed and bound in Hong Kong by
Bookbuilders Ltd

The author

Ray Hutton is an automotive writer and editor, associated with *Car and Driver* in the United States, *Sunday Express Magazine* in England, and a number of car and motor industry journals across Europe, as well as Motor Racing Publications, the publishers of this book.
　He is the Editor of MRP's Enthusiast's Companion series which is designed to provide owners with information and advice to further their enjoyment of interesting modern cars.
　A specialist in the world's motor industry, its products and their design, Ray is Vice President of the international Car of the Year jury. He lives in London and when not testing other people's cars drives his own Porsche 944.

For Z enthusiasts

'We wanted to make a first-class sports car', explained Katsuo Yamada, project leader of the new 300ZX at the time of the car's launch. 'And that means first-class all over the world – in the USA, in Europe and in Japan.'

Nissan's top management recognized and accepted that ambition. The 1989 300ZX was new from stem to stern and shares no more than the name and engine displacement with its predecessor.

They took on the best cars in the world – and succeeded. The new 300ZX not only looks sensational but, in the opinion of some of the industry's harshest critics, matches or surpasses them in all-round excellence.

Not surprisingly, it is attracting discerning owners, many of whom are well educated in high-performance cars. They are, inevitably, enthusiasts. This book is for them.

They will be intrigued to know how Nissan emerged from making some of the world's duller cars to produce a Porsche-challenger. What went into the car's design and development. The secrets of its sophisticated engineering. Who were the key people in making it the way it is. How the various versions – two-seater, 2+2, normally aspirated, Turbo, US and European – perform on road and track. And the background to the Z-car phenomenon which started 20 years before with the Datsun 240Z, the spirit of which has been rekindled in the new-generation 300ZX.

I first became involved with these cars in the 1970s when I was Sports Editor of *Autocar*. That led, indirectly, to writing the MRP Collector's Guide *The Z-series Datsuns* in 1982. The second edition of that book remains in print, as a guide for those who are now able to enjoy the early Zs and ZXs as affordable classics.

The new ZX is something else, as I first discovered in America in the summer of 1989. A preview of the Turbo in Japan that autumn confirmed the car's world class and subsequent experience in the US and in Britain has not changed my mind.

Although this book is about a Nissan, it was not produced for that company. But it would not have been as comprehensive as it is without their help in providing access to people, information and photographs.

As specialist publishers with a fondness for fast cars, we at MRP thought that the story of the new Z-car deserved a book. One which anyone who owns, is thinking of owning, or is just dreaming about a new 300ZX would like to have in their library. Hence this Enthusiast's Companion.

CONTENTS

1. Development of the new 300ZX .... page 6
2. Technical analysis 34
3. Making Nissan's sports car 56
4. Road test – the variants assessed 60
5. Z-car history 78
6. A racing certainty 102

DEVELOPMENT

Objective: world class

What is a sports car? Easy to ask, hard to answer, that was Nissan's starting point for the new 300ZX

The name is the same but the car is completely new. Of course, that's a familiar claim, but in the case of the Nissan 300ZX it is fully justified. Scarcely a component is shared with the car's predecessor, though that was a highly successful model, the last of a line which started with the 1969 Datsun 240Z and developed into the best-selling sports car in history.

Even its best friends accepted that over the years the Z-car had got fat and had lost some of the character of the original. This had not happened by accident, rather as a result of growing up with its main audience in the United States. The 280ZX which followed the original series in 1978 was an intentional move away from the traditional sports car to the personal luxury class. The first 300ZX, which appeared in 1983, was a further development along the same lines.

In 1986 the Nissan Motor Company changed direction. Always Number 2 to Toyota in terms of size, they were losing ground in the Japanese domestic market and were suffering in some of their more important export markets as well. The reasons were many, but the fundamental one was that their products lacked appeal. Nissan made 'safe', unadventurous cars with dull styling and engineering that was no more than 'good enough'. When Yutaka Kume, an engineer who had been in charge of research and development, took over as president in 1985, he promised that things would change.

He saw that they would need to be – and be seen to be – more advanced in design and technology. At the Nissan Technical Centre they initiated Programme 901. That indicated a corporate aim: Number 1 in automotive technology by 1990. It was a tall order, given the standard of their then-current products, but it brought forward some of the more ambitious ideas of Nissan's engineers. Some clues to their future thinking emerged at the 1987 Tokyo Motor Show, where, to the industry's surprise, Nissan presented a stunning array of concept cars. I complimented President Kume on their high standard. He smiled and said that these cars represented Nissan's future: 'We have a new generation of engineers and designers and we have given them their head. We need to attract younger customers, to change our image.'

Those Tokyo Show cars included ARC-X, a prestige saloon car which predicted many of the features of the Nissan's Mercedes challenger, Infiniti Q45, and the second version of the Mid-4 sports car, with a twin-turbo V6 engine and four-wheel drive. We can now see features of the new 300ZX in both.

In terms of production models, the new Z-car was to become the flagship for Nissan's new technology, the car that would prove the '901' concept. It was

Z-car succession – the original 240Z (top) first appeared in 1969; bigger, heavier 280ZX (centre) in 1978; 300ZX (bottom) in 1983.

DEVELOPMENT

clear that this could not be achieved by yet another variation of the existing ZX. When they started work on Project UZ, the new 300ZX, in autumn 1984, the members of Nissan Product Planning Group No 4 (in charge of 'sports-speciality' models) were themselves convinced that it was time for a complete rethink, for a return to the idea which had made the 240Z such a sensation 15 years before.

This was easier said than done. The car world today is infinitely more complicated than the naive 1960s, when a cocktail of existing parts and established styles could be made into a world-beating sports car. It was far from clear what would be the essential elements of such a car for the 1990s. What, indeed, *is* a sports car? There is no unarguable definition, but Nissan's planners had to try to find an answer, for on it would depend the kind of car they would build.

A guiding principle in President Kume's 'new deal' was that all future Nissans should, primarily, provide driving pleasure. Obviously, that was particularly important for a sporting car. Katsuo Yamada, UZ project leader at the time of the launch of the new 300ZX, says that a key point in the planning discussions was the decision that any consideration of a true sports car should start with *performance*.

Just putting these two factors together began to dictate the shape and form of the new Z-car. Shigeyuki Yamaoka, who took Yamada's place as project leader and has been the manager of the Z-car programme since 1982, explains that this was the reason for continuing with a front-engine, rear-drive configuration. The Mid-4 had shown Nissan's thoughts about a mid-engined sports car and some onlookers had predicted this as the way for the new Z, especially since Honda were expected to use such a layout for their future prestige sports car.

Nissan president Yutaka Kume – his appointment changed the company's attitude to advanced engineering.

'We wanted the 300ZX to be enjoyed by a wide spectrum of customers all over the world', says Yamaoka, 'and a high-performance car with a midship engine is appreciated only by those who have higher driving skills. With the "FR" layout we can achieve similarly sharp handling and high-speed stability but with more driving pleasure – for everyone.' Other important considerations were the desire to offer a 2+2 version with occasional rear seats, and the need for reasonable luggage accommodation, neither of which can be provided in a compact mid-engined car.

In early 1985, the existing car which most closely met Nissan's ideals was the Porsche 944 Turbo, but all concerned insist that they did not set out to produce a Japanese copy of a Porsche or anything else; the 944 was there, as a highly-respected sports car, which set standards of performance and handling that they needed to match and, if possible, exceed.

To achieve 944 Turbo performance would need plenty of power – 250–300bhp depending on the weight of the car. The VG30 engine as used in the earlier (Z31) 300ZX was not reckoned to be up to the job, even in its final, Japanese-market, four-cam 24-valve form. So the choice was between a new, or at least heavily revised, V6 of around 3 litres or the recently-developed 4.5-litre V8 of the Infiniti Q45.

Beneath its sleek skin, the new 300ZX is tightly packed with high technology. Nissan's cutaway drawing shows the European specification 300ZX Turbo 2+2.

They decided on the V6 for two reasons. It was more compact and therefore would allow a lower body line. More important, perhaps, was the observation that few new sports cars anywhere in the world exceeded 3–3.5 litres engine capacity and that a big V8 might be seen as profligate at some time in the future. So a new development programme on the VG30 was started – and it ended up virtually creating a new engine. The choice of the V6 also meant that they could offer two versions – normally aspirated and turbocharged.

In view of the Mid-4 and the advanced ATTESA E-TS electronic torque split system of the Skyline GT-R, one might have expected Nissan's technological flagship to have four-wheel drive. 'Of course we considered it,' says Yamaoka, 'but tyres are improving all the time and we knew that thanks to good weight distribution we would have good traction.' Four-wheel drive would undoubtedly have added weight and had an effect on the styling. Yamaoka reckons that the need to accommodate drive-shafts at the front would have raised the bonnet height by at least 2 inches – and that definitely was not desirable.

If this sounds like a closer association between chassis engineers and body designers than is usual in the motor industry, it is so. One effect of President Kume's new way of doing things at the Nissan Technical Centre was to give the project leaders much more authority than hitherto. They were made responsible not only for the design and engineering of a new model but also for the sales and marketing plans. Previously, key decisions about styling and market positioning were taken at top management level. Now the project leader carries the can. Katsuo Yamada, since promoted to a new job at Nissan in North America, and Shigeyuki Yamaoka, take – and deserve – the credit for the new 300ZX.

Identity parade

There was a lot of debate within Nissan about the naming of Project UZ. The car was completely different from the first 300ZX, which had logically derived from the 280ZX when the 3-litre V6 engine was fitted. Shouldn't it, therefore, have a different name?

Some people thought so. Since the declared aim was to interpret the values of the original Datsun 240Z for buyers in the 1990s, they favoured 300Z for the new model. In the end, according to Katsuo Yamada, it was decided to continue with the familiar model designation as it followed the NX, SX theme of other models in the Nissan range: 'We figured that the customers would soon find out how different the new car is.'

In Japan, the Datsun 240Z was called the Nissan Fairlady Z, a designation that is still used today for the new 300ZX. Fairlady was one of a series of whimsical names introduced by Nissan's president in the 1960s; it reflected his enjoyment of the musical 'My Fair Lady'.

In the early 1980s Nissan decided to drop Datsun and adopt the company name for their cars worldwide. For the 300ZX in Japan, the 'Z' motif takes prominence over the maker's name and is carried in the round emblem on the nose. Cars for Europe have a Nissan badge instead, but US-market 300ZXs have no badge on the nose panel at all – though there is discreet Nissan lettering above the air intake.

DEVELOPMENT

Project leaders – Katsuo Yamada (right) had plenty to smile about at the 300ZX launch, while Shigeyuki Yamaoka (far right) continues the serious business of Z-car development in Product Planning & Marketing Department No 4 at Nissan Technical Centre.

Nissan Mid-4 prototype was rumoured to herald ZX successor but is now in abeyance as a production version was thought too expensive.

Consideration was given to using the V8 engine from the Infiniti Q45 saloon and also to selling the new 300ZX through Nissan's newly-created prestige channel in the USA.

300ZX

'Every generation has its own shape of sports car,' says Yoshio Maezawa, deputy general manager of the Nissan Design Centre. 'In the 1960s, it was the long-bonnet, short-tail style. The shape of the 1990s is set by Group C and IMSA GTP sports-racing cars.' He refers to a pushed-forward look with a short nose, long windscreen and 'coke bottle' body curvature. Not surprisingly, you can see it in the new 300ZX.

In Nissan parlance, Maezawa is a design producer, rather in the sense of a film producer. He controls and co-ordinates all the elements of a new design and represents the Design Centre in negotiations with the project leader and higher management.

Everyone involved realized that the shape and style of the new 300ZX would be crucial to its success. When it was decided to start Project UZ with a clean sheet of paper, they had no preconceived ideas of how it should look. All they knew was that it had to be distinctive – and be able to create an excitement equivalent to that made when the 240Z was introduced.

There was not – and is not – a specific Z design team, though the studio managers were able to select a group of five exterior and four interior designers who have a particular flair for this kind of car. As is usual in the bigger manufacturers, there was a competition between individual designers to decide on the best approach. Unlike some, no external consultancy was involved, though Nissan Design International in San Diego, California, was to make one of the competitive proposals.

The new car was planned to be a more international product than its predecessor, which was tailored expressly for the American market. But the majority of sales would continue to be in the US, so it was important that the

Though Nissan have the latest in computer design aids, the 300ZX shape was arrived at through conventional sketching and modelling.

Starting points – renderings produced at the concept stage, some showing ideas for the final form.

designers involved fully understood the environment in which it would be used.

So, at the outset, two Japanese designers were sent to the US West Coast on what could be described as a style-finding mission. One of them was Isao Sono, manager of exterior design in Nissan's Studio No 1. He returned certain of one thing, that the design had to have a very strong character. It needed to be bold enough to stand out at a distance; perspectives in America's wide open spaces and straight freeways were very different from the congested streets of Japan.

An early decision about the car's dimensions had an important bearing on achieving a modern but distinctive style. Accommodation had to be equivalent to the existing 300ZX, but it was agreed that outwardly the car should be smaller. The result was a significant (5.2in) increase in wheelbase, but a reduction in overall length. The longer wheelbase and shorter overhangs automatically encouraged the 'cab forward' stance that research had suggested.

From hundreds of sketches and renderings like those shown here, 11 ideas were selected to be worked up into one-fifth scale models. A thorough review then put forward three to be built as full-size mock-ups, externally complete in every detail. These were 'cliniced' inside and outside the company, involving not only design staff and management but employees from other areas, young university students, and dealers and automotive journalists from the USA.

We can see from the full-size models shown opposite that the final choice was of the most radical design, which originated in the Design Centre in Japan as the work of Isao Sono and Toshio Yamashita. Nissan's design managers usually expect NDI in California to produce the wildest ideas, but not in this case. They admit that the San Diego studio's subsequent involvement in developing the new 300ZX is 'a delicate issue' but, officially, the final product was a co-operative effort.

What are the special features of the chosen design? Sono explains: 'We wanted to place the driver at the centre of the car, between the front and rear wheels, to achieve a visual balance. We made the side windows very characteristic, and of course the steeply raked windscreen and unusual headlamps add to its personality.'

Both the screen and the lamps pushed Nissan's suppliers to the limit. Yoshio Maezawa says that while Ferrari and Lamborghini might be able to get away with a screen rake of less than 25deg, to achieve the 26deg that they wanted without distortion and in high volume was quite an achievement. Similarly, without the co-operation of Ichiko Kogyo, the lamp supplier, who developed a new glass-pressing process, they could not have had headlights of the unique shape and angle they required.

With the car's high performance objectives, good aerodynamics was obviously important for stability and Toshio Yamashita worked closely with the wind-tunnel specialists to refine the chosen shape: 'We set a Cd (drag coefficient) target, but kept the emphasis on styling. Cars with a good Cd don't necessarily look good.' They were happy to achieve a Cd of 0.31 for the

DEVELOPMENT

Final choice was between these three full-size mock-ups. The top one has an unusual rear window treatment and heavy centre pillars. At centre is the proposal from the NDI studio in California with glassy cabin and concealed headlamps. At the bottom is the design finally chosen, developed at NTC in Japan. Later modifications were made to the angle of the headlamps, the panel between them, and the rear quarter windows.

17

Assessing design proposals out of doors is an important part of the review process. Above, models exemplify the old and new sports car stance – long-bonnet and cab-forward, mid-engine styles.

The unusual headlamps, which are set at a 60-degree angle, were a key feature of the final style. They incorporate a miniature projector lens for low-beam.

normally aspirated car and to have a lift coefficient close to zero, front and rear.

It became clear, however, that the faster Turbo model would need a deeper front apron and a tail spoiler, even if these increased drag. While accepting the functional requirement, the designers prefer the 'pure' form of the normally aspirated car.

Interestingly, at no stage in the planning and design process was any serious consideration given to a 300ZX convertible, though it was accepted that removable roof panels would be offered (in fact, very few cars were to be made without them). This influenced the window design, for the doors could have no upper frame.

Two-seater and 2+2 versions were planned all along, and although the original designs were of the shorter car, they managed to achieve a very close visual similarity between the two. There is a 5in. difference between the trailing edge of the door and the rear wheelarch, but you scarcely notice it. Producer Maezawa allows his studio a rare piece of self-congratulation: 'In a situation like

The three design finalists reviewed at an early stage at the San Diego studio, with the NDI fifth-scale model photographed with the two others in full-size. Note that all three were developed further before being presented as shown on page 17.

this, usually one of the designs has to be sacrificed. This time it wasn't. This was very successful.'

Overall, Nissan's designers are pleased with themselves about the 300ZX. Owing nothing to outside agencies or cars that have gone before, it represents a new confidence for Japanese car design. Yoshio Maezawa likes to talk of a fusion of delicacy and sophistication, as exemplified by Japanese art, and *kyojin*, a steel-like inner strength represented by a sword in Japanese dance. But he is keen to emphasize that the styling must have global appeal: 'I want people to regard it first as good, and then secondly as Japanese.'

Whilst we can see similarities in the frontal treatment, the curvature of the cabin, and the window line between the ARC-X concept car and the new 300ZX, they were, in fact, handled by quite different people. There was a closer association with the team that produced the new 200/240SX, as that project was developed in the Design Centre in parallel with its bigger brother.

Though not everyone likes its expanse of moulded plastic, the 200/240SX

Wind tunnel testing involved a number of detail trade-offs to achieve target drag and lift coefficients, but the designers' basic shape remained unaltered. Final Cd values were 0.31 for the normally aspirated car and 0.32 for the bespoilered Turbo.

interior can be seen to have led the way to the new 300ZX. Further back in time, we can see the influence of the Porsche 928 in creating a twin 'cockpit' effect, enclosing driver and passenger by the sweep of facia, centre console and door trim.

An exciting layout for a sports car, it is rather like two single-seater racing cars side-by-side. It is both practical and attractive to look at and eschews the gimmicks that, increasingly, had marked earlier ZXs.

So there are no digital instruments or Tokyo-by-night electronic displays here. Kazuo Sugisima, the manager in charge of furnishing the new 300ZX, says that, just like the concept of the car itself, the interior was completely rethought: 'We went back to basics and asked what a true sports car instrument panel should be like. This is a car that can be driven very fast, so the visibility of the panel has to be very good and controls logically placed near to the steering wheel.'

The hooded binnacle contains large, clear, white-on-black analog instruments, and pods either side of the wheel place all essential driving switchgear scarcely more than a finger-span away. Unlike the Porsche 928, which has a somewhat

DEVELOPMENT

The team that shaped the new 300ZX – from left to right, Toshio Yamashita, who took the design from scale to full-size model; Kazuo Sugisima, responsible for the interior; Yoshio Maezawa, design producer; and Isao Sono, who created the car's style.

Though there are similarities in frontal treatment, roof and window line between the 300ZX and this ARC-X concept car, they were produced by different design teams.

300ZX

similar arrangement, the column and the binnacle are not adjustable. Sugisima says that it does not need to be, since they have paid careful attention to the eyeline of drivers of different heights and provided a wide range of seat adjustment so that everyone can set an appropriate driving position.

Certainly, there is no lack of space for the driver and front seat passenger. The individual cockpit idea is best exemplified by the 300ZX two-seater, where the thick-weave tweed fabric trim forms an elliptical surround to each passenger space, from armrests on the doors, across the lower part of the facia, down the centre console, to join the ledge of the luggage area. With the standard trim, the same cloth is used on the seats themselves, which makes for a harmonious appearance. The optional leather-covered seats tone with the black mouldings of the facia and door tops and the control surfaces.

It is a well-planned interior where everything looks as if it belongs and there are no out-of-place add-ons. The sweeping curves echo the shape of the outside. Earlier proposals which were more angular and made the centre console part of the instrument and control area did not suit the body style so well.

If lengthening the wheelbase has increased the cabin space in the front, it has not done much for the rear passengers in the 2+2, who still need to be either very small or prepared to put up with considerable discomfort. But with the backrest folded down this version does have usefully more luggage space than the two-seater.

While Nissan's product planners were agonizing over what makes up a sports car, in the Vehicle Development Department they were also doing some soul-

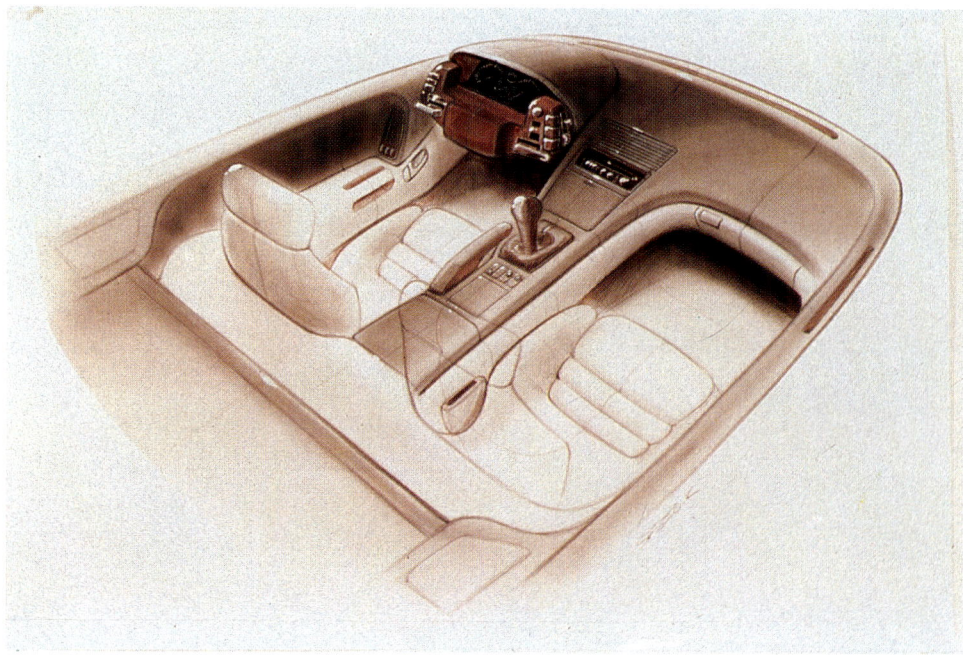

Concept sketch for the interior shows thinking for an elliptical 'cockpit' configuration and hooded instrument/ control binnacle.

Development of the cabin – seating 'bucks' were built to show exactly how proposals would look. The deeply hooded control module, centre, and the more conventional, angular facia above, were rejected in favour of sweeping curves, below.

searching. Did they, the company's test drivers, really have the skills and appreciation of cars with near-racecar potential?

Having the idea of producing a thoroughbred sports car was one thing, reproducing the all-round performance and feel of the world's finest was quite another. Nissan had very experienced testers, but they worked mostly at the company's three proving grounds. 'Target cars' – in this case, notably Porsche 944, 928 and Chevrolet Corvette – were available to them, but they were aware that the everyday use of these cars in other countries was very different from test tracks or road conditions in Japan.

So, as part of the clean-sheet development approach, the new 300ZX became the first Nissan to have an extensive overseas test programme. The manager of the Vehicle Development Department No 1, Motoo Yanagawa, explains the rationale: 'Japan is a very limited environment. We don't drive very hard on the public roads here. Conditions are different in the USA and in Europe. The objective of our overseas test programme was to check whether the car was acceptable in those conditions; in a sense, to confirm its citizenship.'

Before that, though, it was decided to expand the experience of a selected group of test drivers. They were sent to the ADAC Rennsport race driving school at the old 14-mile Nurburgring in Germany, not to learn to race (which none of them do) but to develop their judgmental skills by driving a variety of high-performance cars at the limit on this very demanding circuit. They also drove Porsche 944s and 928s at high speed on the autobahn and were surprised to discover that Europeans also had many opportunities to drive fast on winding roads. They travelled in the US, re-evaluating the old 300ZX in the light of ambitions for the new one, assessing rival cars, and learning why so many American enthusiasts love the Corvette, which seems so cumbersome in Europe or Japan. The tricky Laguna Seca and Willow Springs race tracks in California were added to their test programme.

'What we learnt from the target cars was not about technology, but about product philosophy', says Yanagawa. 'We concluded that a sports car should have safety as a pre-condition and, based on that, should always respond faithfully to a driver's input and meet his expectations. Furthermore, when we thought about a *modern* sports car, we saw no reason to compromise on things like ride comfort and noise. High-output engines used to concentrate on top-end power. We thought that a modern sports car should not be like this, that it should be able to offer a blend of high performance, good handling and stability, and a comfortable, civilized ride.'

Quite so. Having defined the task and equipped themselves with the means of assessing the result, all they had to do was produce a chassis that could do the job. The Vehicle Development people work closely with the Chassis Design Department, particularly at the concept stage. 'We decided at an early stage that the MacPherson-strut front and semi-trailing-arm rear suspension would not be good enough for the new 300ZX', recalls Koumei Yazaki, one of Nissan's elite

DEVELOPMENT

Nissan Technical Centre has considerable CAD (Computer Aided Design) resources, including two Cray supercomputers, which were used in the development of the 300ZX chassis.

testers, whose job description is 'senior specialist in chassis development'.

The kind of more sophisticated suspension to be adopted was, in effect, decided by the broader 901 programme. Nissan were developing a number of powerful front-engine, rear-wheel drive cars – the 200/240SX, the new Skyline and the Infiniti Q45 – all of which would face similar problems. A multi-link rear suspension system was devised, similar in some respects to that used by Mercedes-Benz. It appeared first on the ARC-X and Mid-4 concept cars and made its production debut on the 200/240Z in 1988.

Nevertheless, the engineers working on the UZ project, headed by Yuuichi Sanada, analyzed several different layouts for the front and rear suspension. They had two secret weapons. One was a Cray X/MP supercomputer which could handle highly complex mathematical simulations at lightning speed. For a car manufacturer, a Cray is a kind of macho symbol, partly because they cost so much ($20 million) but also because only the very best-equipped tech centres have them. Hence they tend to display them with pride whenever they have the opportunity. Nissan now have two. On a recent visit, one well-travelled journalist said, 'there are only six of these in the world's motor industry and I've seen 10 of them...'.

These mighty computers certainly speeded up the analysis and allowed the engineers to narrow down the options to a few that were promising enough to be built experimentally. At that stage they were helped by the second secret

Computers can do the groundwork, but there comes a time when all suspension designs have to be tested for real, hence this STB (Suspension Test Bed), an adjustable chassis used to evaluate suspension systems and variations of weight, track and wheelbase.

weapon, the STB, or Suspension Test Bed. This looks rather like a backyard hotrod, but in fact is a sophisticated piece of equipment, made up of three modules. The turbocharged V6 engine is mounted with the driver's seat in the centre one. Front and rear modules can be changed or adjusted so that different suspension geometry, wheelbase, track and weight distributions can be tried on the test track.

Finally, they arrived at a multi-link system for both front and rear of the 300ZX and could use the same principles for the Skyline and Infiniti. In the case of Project UZ, the next step was to adapt some old 300ZXs to the new hardware. These were important prototypes as they could be used for durability tests on normal roads without the danger of being snapped by a spy photographer and having the new model exposed prematurely in the world's press. Later, for the same reason, some prototypes with the complete new chassis had old 300ZX panels tacked on.

Though four-wheel drive and active suspension, both being worked on for other cars, were rejected for the 300ZX, mainly on the grounds of bulk and weight, the engineers were keen to incorporate their latest thinking in four-wheel steering. This is called Super HICAS (for High Capacity Actively Controlled Suspension) and is integrated with the multi-link rear suspension system. It is described in detail in the next chapter. Suffice to say here that the limited rear steering is designed to improve the car's behaviour in a swerve at high speed and was therefore incorporated as standard equipment on the 300ZX Turbo.

The complete UZ test programme took three years and involved 190 prototype cars and a total of 1.25 million miles. At the end of it, the designers

DEVELOPMENT

and development engineers were satisfied that they had produced a true sports car that, without compromise, could meet the different market conditions all over the world. That is not to say that the 300ZX is the same in all countries. In fact, there are eight different specifications which vary considerably, but only in detail – in spring rates, damper type and setting, tyre size and type, and even the electronic control of Super HICAS.

Ace tester Yazaki was one of the team of five development drivers who carried out this fine-tuning, having concluded that American customers would prefer stiffer suspension than Europeans and quicker steering response – hence, for the US 300ZX Turbo, two-position shock absorbers, a higher steering ratio and lower speed actuation of Super HICAS. According to Yazaki, the European version sacrifices just a little in low-speed response for improved stability nearer the maximum. Having lived with the 300ZX and the best of its competitors (like the rock-steady Porsche 928S4) over hundreds of miles of autobahn testing, Yazaki says, 'I am confident that in terms of high-speed stability our car is the best in the world'.

Moreover, the European-specification 300ZX Turbo lapped the tortuous Nurburgring in 8min 40sec – some 6 seconds faster than Porsche's top test driver Gunther Steckkonig could manage in a 928GT in an exercise run by the magazine *Auto Bild* to find the fastest German production car.

So the 300ZX was ready. The US launch was scheduled for the Chicago Auto Show in February 1989, where it appeared labelled as a 1990 model, though it went on sale from May 1. Only the 222bhp normally aspirated two-seater

For reasons of security and convenience, much of the testing of the new 300ZX chassis was done with these prototypes wearing bodywork from the previous Z31 model.

Design and test team – Yuuichi Sanada, right, is the manager of the chassis design department responsible for the 300ZX multi-link suspension, while Koumei Yazaki, left, was one of Nissan's elite team of specially trained test drivers who developed the car in its various specifications.

The new body shape also had to be tested in real-world conditions – this 'mule' has the key panels of the new 300ZX grafted on to an old shell.

DEVELOPMENT

appeared at first. The 2+2 followed in June and the 300bhp Turbo (two-seater only in the US) in September. Nissan in the USA expected the Turbo to take only 15% of 300ZX sales; the normally aspirated two-seater accounts for 50%.

All versions are sold in Japan, but unlike previous Z-cars there is no 2-litre option for the home market; a change in the tax rules meant that a smaller-engined version was no longer so advantageous. The normally aspirated 300ZX was introduced in Australia in November. By then Nissan had decided that only one model would be homologated for Europe – the 300ZX Turbo 2+2. This would go on sale in spring 1990; in the UK from April 1.

At the Z-car factory, Nissan Shatai in Hiratsuka City, near Yokohama, production was set at 5,000 cars per month. More than half of these were destined for the United States. It immediately became the top seller in its class, though at a lower sales rate than the previous ZX had enjoyed at its peak. That reflects the new model's significantly higher price. A return to the values of the original 240Z could not include its bargain price. The new 300ZX started at $27,900, rising to over $35,000 for a fully-equipped Turbo.

In Japan, the new model did better than any previous Z. Nissan Motor and Prince dealers sold 2,000 300ZXs a month in the first six months – four times the number of its predecessor. Prices between 3.2 and 4.5 million yen (approximately equivalent to £12,500–£17,500) are high by Japanese standards, so it is not surprising that most buyers are identified as 'DINKIES' (Double Income, No Kids)!

On the UK market, the 300ZX achieved the slightly doubtful distinction of becoming the most expensive – as well as the fastest – Japanese car ever offered. The Turbo 2+2 fully 'loaded' except for automatic transmission and leather upholstery, which remained extra-cost options, entered at £34,500.

Though some expressed concern about its price, the 300ZX received fulsome praise in reviews published all over the world. Inevitably, wheel-to-wheel comparisons were made with Porsches and Corvettes; most were favourable towards the new Nissan. The conclusions of some of these are included in Chapter 3.

Motor Trend named the 300ZX Turbo 1990 Import Car of the Year – a significant accolade since the contest also included such highly regarded newcomers as the Mercedes 500SL, the Mazda Miata MX-5, the Toyota Lexus LS400, Nissan's own Infiniti Q45, and the new version of America's best-selling car, the Honda Accord.

Naturally, Nissan were proud to win the award. But perhaps even more of the magazine's summing-up of their work: 'Dollar for dollar, the 300ZX is the best damn sports car in the world.'

The finished product – 300ZX Turbo two-seater shines in the California sun.

300ZX

European-specification 300ZX Turbo 2+2 was displayed at international motor shows in Frankfurt, London and Geneva before going on sale in spring 1990.

Image-making in Japan – the Fairlady Z has elaborate brochures, postcards and even a pictorial telephone credit card. Domestic sales far exceed the car's predecessor.

DEVELOPMENT

Presentation time – Robert Thomas, vice president of Nissan Motor Corporation in USA, accepts Motor Trend's Import Car of the Year award from Robert Brown, senior vice president of Petersen Publishing, at the 1990 Chicago Auto Show.

Though Nissan reject the idea of a 300ZX Convertible, such cars are being produced by specialist coachbuilders. This is the first: the PPG Pace Car designed and built by ASC in California. It has a 400bhp turbo engine and was used as a pace car at 1989 CART Indy-car races.

Talking technical

Nissan aimed for leadership in technology with the new 300ZX as its flagship. A detailed look at its innovations

Nissan Technical Centre at Atsugi, on a good day about an hour's drive from Tokyo, has an air of secrecy. The firmly but politely policed security gate is 100 yards or so in front of an escarpment pierced by two single-track access tunnels. Some 4,000 people work on the other side of the hill. For the last four years of the Eighties they were spurred on by programme '901'. The new 300ZX is seen as the flagship for that technology, and working on its development was regarded as a high honour by the engineers involved.

Nissan have put a massive investment behind NTC, but the resources are not unlimited. Faced, for example, with the simple statement that the new Z-car should have 'the world's best sports car engine for the 1990s', the engine design department might have chosen to start from scratch, but that wasn't possible. 'We didn't have time to develop a totally new engine', explains senior engineer Masataka Nakajima. 'We might have liked to have an aluminium cylinder block, for example, but the constraint was development time – and the cost and complexity of production.'

Having considered, but rejected, the use of the Infiniti VH45 V8, they were therefore committed to a further development of the VG30 3-litre 60-degree V6. When they came to decide what would be required of the world's best sports car engine they focussed on three objectives: high power output – ideally, 100bhp per litre – but with ample torque in the low and medium speed range; excellent throttle response and exceptional smoothness for good driveability; and good reliability in all types of driving conditions.

The starting point was the VG30DE variant, the four-cam, 24-valve engine offered only in the Japanese market in the closing years of the previous 300ZX. That had an maximum output of 190bhp in normally aspirated form and with a single turbocharger could produce 255bhp. Comparable figures for the 12-valve engines were 170 (n/a) and 225 (Turbo) in European specification (without catalytic convertor) and 160 and 205bhp for the USA.

Both the normally aspirated and turbocharged engines required for the new car had to be substantially more powerful than these predecessors. With the same cubic capacity, that meant that the engine would have to run faster than the 5,400–5,600rpm maximum of the old unit. And that, in turn, dictated modifications which became so comprehensive that they virtually amounted to a new engine.

The two versions were developed in parallel and, where possible, share common parts. The basic over-square cylinder dimensions remain as before, as does the bore pitch, so that the cast-iron block can continue to be made on the

ANALYSIS

Cutaway drawing of the VG30DETT engine shows a 60-degree vee cylinder configuration, turbocharger placement low down either side of the engine and twin intercoolers. Twin intake manifolds crossover to opposite cylinder banks. Cylinder heads (right) have classic four-valve-per-cylinder layout with twin overhead camshafts per bank and pent-roof combustion chambers with symmetrically placed valves and central spark plugs.

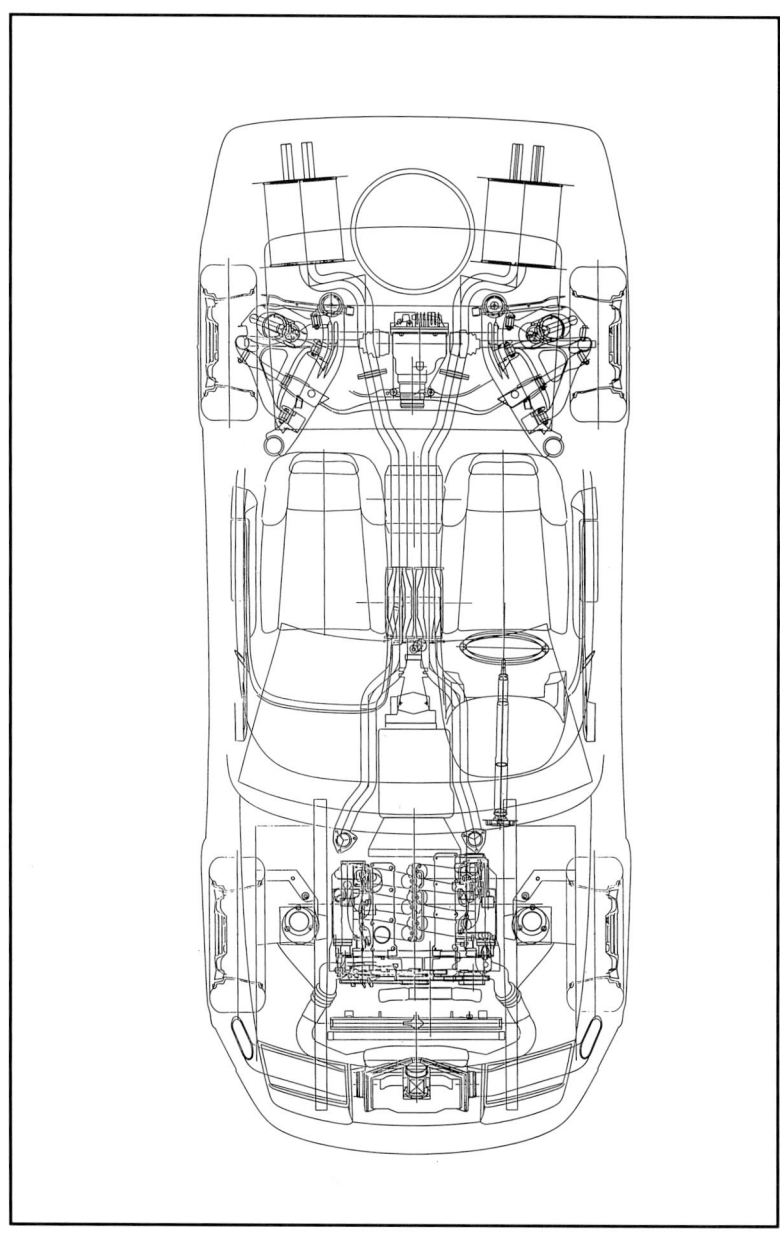

Plan of mechanical layout shows something of the impressive packaging of the relatively short engine bay, and the accommodation of the multi-link suspension systems.

same production lines. But even that is not without changes, for by using thinner sections with rib reinforcements it has been made both stiffer and some 4.5lb lighter than the earlier block.

The basic internals are new – a forged crankshaft replaces the previous casting, and the pistons and the connecting rods are of a new design. Pistons for the 300ZX Turbo are different again, with differently shaped crowns (the compression ratio of the Turbo is lower, at 8.5:1) and special oil channels for cooling. Con-rod bearings for the Turbo are made of Kelmet, a high-strength copper/lead alloy widely used in racing engines.

The aluminium alloy cylinder heads are similar to but modified from those of the earlier VG30DE. The combustion chambers have the classic four-valves-per-

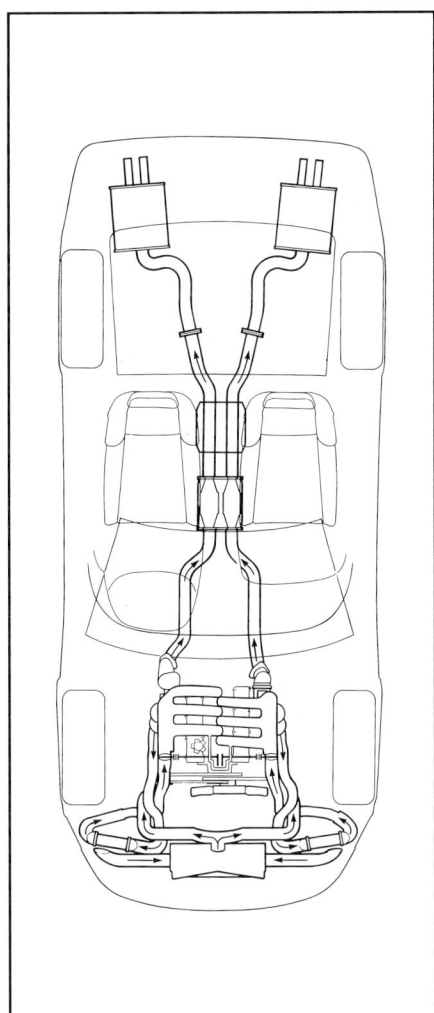
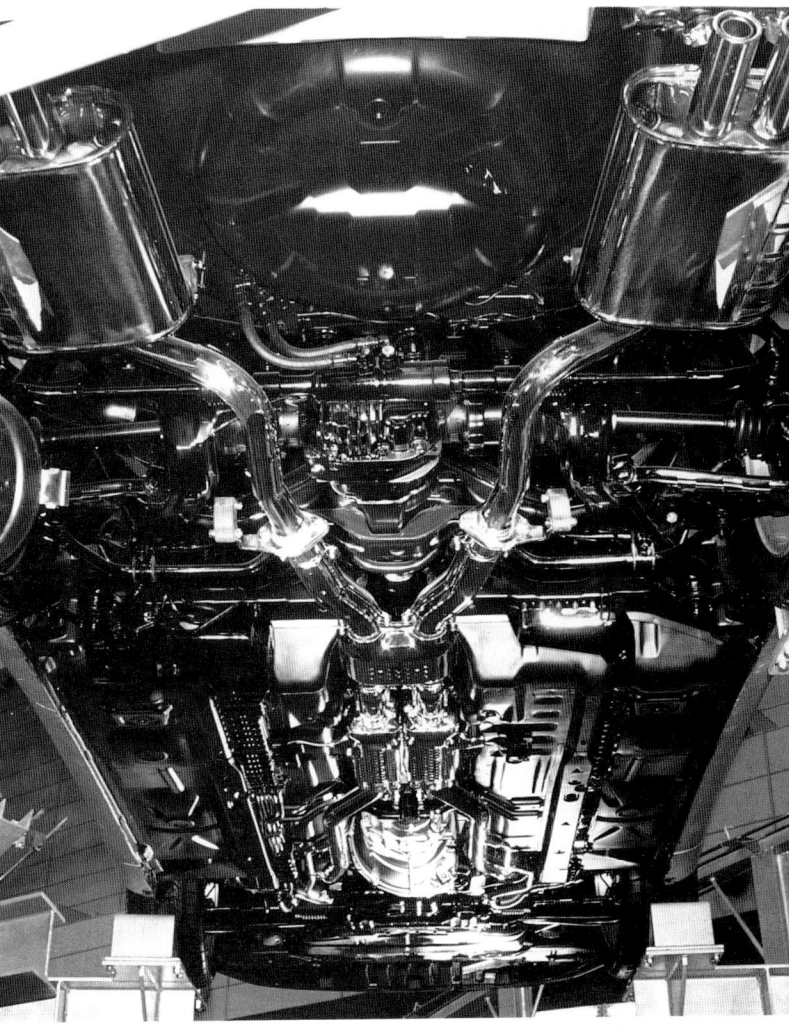

The engineers responsible regard the plumbing of the dual intake and exhaust systems in the 300ZX Turbo as one of their greater achievements. Compare with the photograph taken of the underside of a specially prepared show car.

cylinder layout with the pairs of valves symmetrically disposed within a pent-roof and a centrally placed spark plug. The valves themselves are the same size as before – inlets slightly bigger than exhausts. To cope with the Turbo's higher temperatures, its exhaust valves are made of Iconel, a tough aircraft-grade steel.

Twin overhead camshafts for each bank of cylinders provide the most efficient, direct way of operating the valves and they do so via self-adjusting hydraulic tappets.

Thus far, this is pretty standard stuff for a modern high performance engine. But the 300ZX does have several novel features. The workings of the direct ignition and variable valve timing are described on the next pages. The illustrations on this spread show the sheer complexity of the external pipe systems.

Each cylinder bank has independent inlet and exhaust systems. This is desirable for gasflow, but so would be short inlet tracts, and on the ZX the pipework is long and convoluted. It had to be to fit under the low bonnet. Masataka Nakajima says that the 'packaging' of the intake system is the aspect of the engine of which the engineers are most proud.

Not much space to spare under the bonnet of the 300ZX Turbo. A finisher plate between the inlet manifolds covers throttle linkages. The twin turbochargers are hidden from view, mounted low, either side of the engine.

It is, indeed, a masterpiece of plumbing – all the more so in the Turbo which has to direct inlet air from the single front-mounted air cleaner back to the turbochargers either side of the engine and then forward again to the intercoolers in the nose and back to the so-called cross-ram manifolds, feeding to the opposite cylinder bank.

The exhaust is a true dual system from engine to twin tailpipes, with catalytic convertors either side of the car's centreline under the seats. The Turbo also has small supplementary catalysts built into the downpipes which heat up quickly to ensure catalytic action directly after a cold start.

So the 300ZX Turbo has twin inlets, twin throttles, twin exhausts and twin turbochargers. Previous Z Turbos have used only one turbocharger. There was a layout logic in fitting two on the new one, but mostly the decision was dictated by the desire to achieve a high power output and good low and mid-range response.

Two turbochargers mean that each can be smaller, and thus have less inertial mass, so that it spins more readily. This reduces 'turbo lag', the irritating delay between the driver pressing the throttle and the engine providing boosted performance. In achieving the optimum size, Nissan engineers chose a hybrid of Garrett AiResearch turbochargers – the exhaust-driven turbine from the small T2 with the air compressor of the larger T25. In common with other Japanese manufacturers, Nissan have developed lightweight ceramic turbocharger rotors and used them in production cars, including a domestic-market version of the old 300ZX. But with the smaller turbines of the twin-turbo installation they could achieve their performance goals without such space-age components. The over-boost control system is also kept simple, using mechanical wastegates instead of complicated electronics.

ANALYSIS

Turbochargers generate a great deal of external heat. This dictated a big temperature-sensitive cooling fan that operates at three different speeds. It also meant using cast-iron exhaust manifolds instead of the stainless steel ones found on the normally aspirated version. Another consideration was preventing fuel vaporization after engine shut-down, which can make hot-starting difficult with turbo engines. Nissan's solution was to increase the fuel pressure and to fit a vacuum-operated regulator device to keep it constant under all conditions.

Other developments with reliability in mind concerned the lubrication system. The Turbo has an engine oil cooler as standard, which has a bypass system operated at high rpm. An unexpected problem arose when serious track testing started with the new car; it was capable of generating much higher cornering forces than its predecessor, which caused oil surge in the sump, lubricant starvation, and engine damage. A new oil pan with a different shape and baffles had to be designed.

The electronic heart of the 300ZX engine is the ECCS management computer. ECCS stands for Electronic Concentrated Control System and is a modular system used in a wide range of Nissan vehicles. In the 300ZX, apart from directing the sequential electronic fuel injection, it also looks after the operation

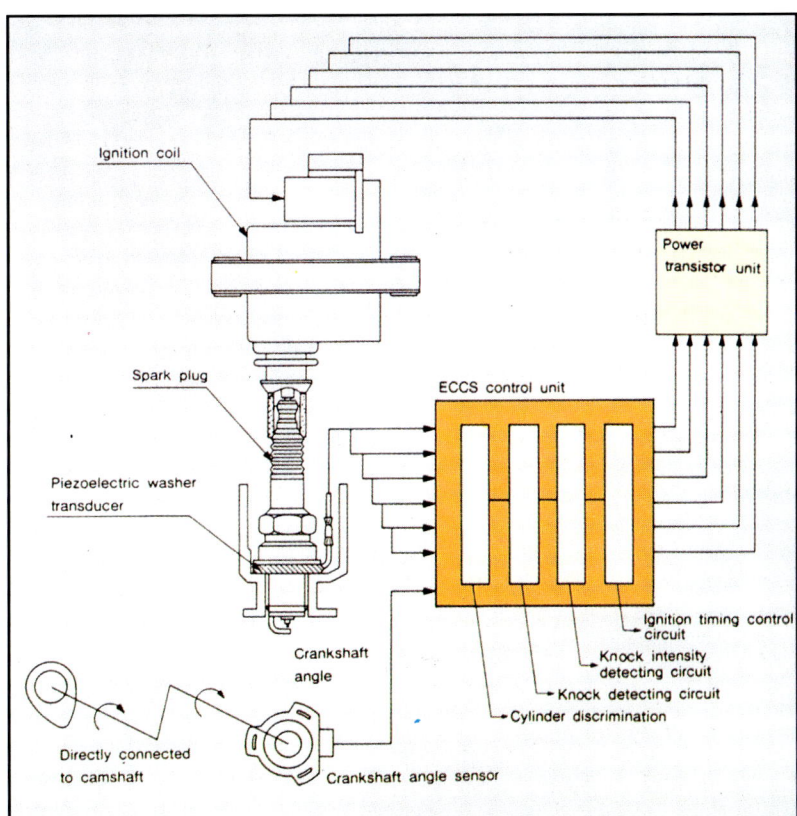

NDIS – Nissan Direct Ignition System – provides a miniature coil for each sparking plug, controlled by the engine management computer.

of the innovative NDIS (Nissan Direct Ignition System) and NVCS (Nissan Valve Timing Control System) both of which were incorporated early in the development and make an important contribution to the engines' impressive all-round performance. Nissan were not the first to use direct ignition – Saab showed it some years before and have been fitting it for some time on their Turbo models. It is an elegant arrangement, dispensing with coil, distributor and the volt-sapping high-tension cables running between them. With direct ignition, each spark plug has a miniature coil mounted above it and clipped directly to it. The ECCS responds to a sensor on the crankshaft to send a signal to each cylinder in turn, telling the mini-coil to transform current transmitted direct from the transistor ignition pack into secondary current for the plug. The advantage over a conventional system is that it eliminates the voltage drop that can occur through the distributor and HT leads at high rpm.

Variable valve timing is not unique either – Alfa Romeo produced a four-cylinder with it in the early 1980s and it is a feature of the latest Mercedes-Benz SL model and the remarkably powerful Honda V-TEC engines. Honda's system works on both the inlet and exhaust timing, but Nissan's NVCS is like the Alfa and Mercedes systems in operating only on the inlet camshaft. Before the 300ZX, Nissan introduced it on Cedric and Leopard models.

The proposition for variable valve timing is this: valve timing that allows the engine to 'breathe' easily at high speed, to the advantage of maximum power, is usually less satisfactory at low speeds. Fixed timing is, inevitably, a compromise. High-performance sports car engines have always tended towards 'top end' power, sacrificing low and mid-range torque. Driveability, fuel consumption and exhaust emissions suffer. Timing of the opening and closing of valves by the camshaft is measured by degrees of crankshaft rotation. If the camshaft position

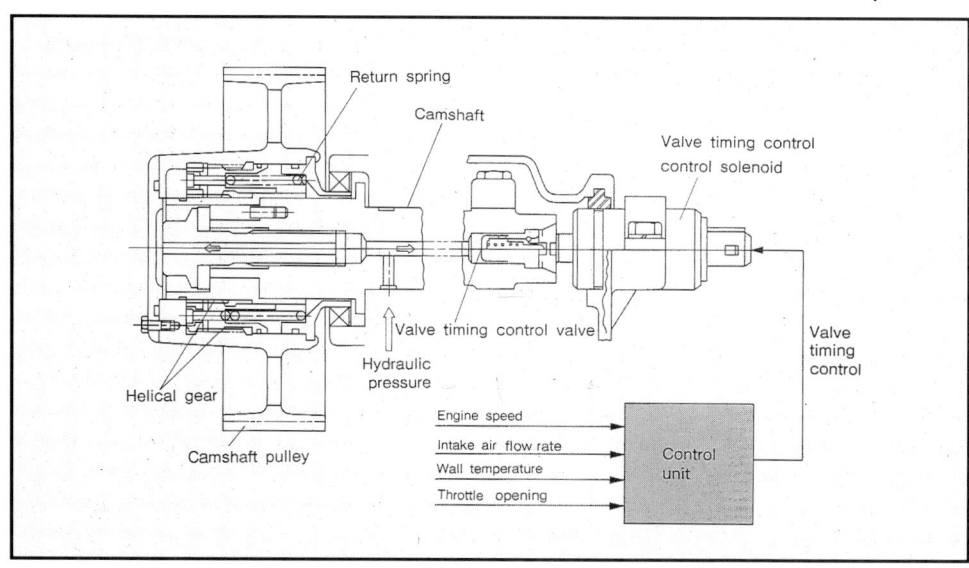

How NVCS, Nissan's variable valve timing system, works. The timing of the inlet camshafts is advanced by 10 degrees at low speed.

can be altered with engine speed and load, it can deliver optimal timing for low-speed smoothness and efficiency *and* maximum output at high rpm.

In Nissan's case this is achieved by rotating a helical gear interposed between the cam pulley and the camshaft itself. Thus, at low speed and light load, the inlet valves can be closed earlier to reduce 'overlap' with the exhaust valve opening, to improve the torque characteristics, while at high speed the interval can be extended for the best 'breathing'.

In NVCS the rotation of the spring-loaded helical gear at the cam pulley is achieved hydraulically, but it does of course depend on electronic control. The ECCS computer reacts to signals of engine rpm, intake airflow, throttle position and temperature to operate a solenoid which releases hydraulic pressure. It is a two-position rather than fully variable system and the basic position is for high-speed efficiency; NVCS is therefore brought into operation at low speeds.

Variable timing was important in achieving the 300ZX's performance objectives, for without it, low-speed running behaviour would probably not have been acceptable. As it was, they were able to reach 300bhp at 6,400rpm with the Turbo and 222bhp at the same speed for the normally aspirated engine – even the latter was a considerable improvement on the previous 12-valve 300ZX Turbo. Maximum torque was well up, too – 283lb/ft at 3,600rpm for the Turbo and 198lb/ft at 4,800rpm, normally aspirated.

These figures are with full US/Japan emissions control equipment including three-way catalytic convertors and exhaust gas recirculation. For various reasons, the 300ZX Turbo in some versions is rated at 280bhp. This applies to the Japanese domestic market, where the manufacturers have an agreement to limit outputs to 280, to automatic-transmission models in the US, which have different camshaft profiles and fuel injection settings, and to the European market 2+2 because of its setting for lower-octane unleaded fuel.

Shifting standards

Worldwide there are not too many manual gearboxes available that can handle up to 300lb/ft of torque. For the previous 300ZX Turbo, Nissan had started with a Borg-Warner design, a tough transmission used in a number of US high-performance cars. For the new car, the engineering effort concentrated on refinement and shift quality.

As in other areas, their initial research was remarkably thorough. They assessed a whole range of sporting cars on the basis of the precision and ease of movement of the gearshift. Toshimasa Doi, manager of manual transmission design at NTC, shows a graph which rates them all and the previous Z-car has a circle indicating unfavourable comment. The same assessment carried out more recently puts the new 300ZX among the very best, beaten only by the Mazda Miata MX-5, which has an altogether lighter transmission.

What made the difference was the use of double cone synchronizers and a rethink of the position and actuation of the gearlever. Their analysis concluded

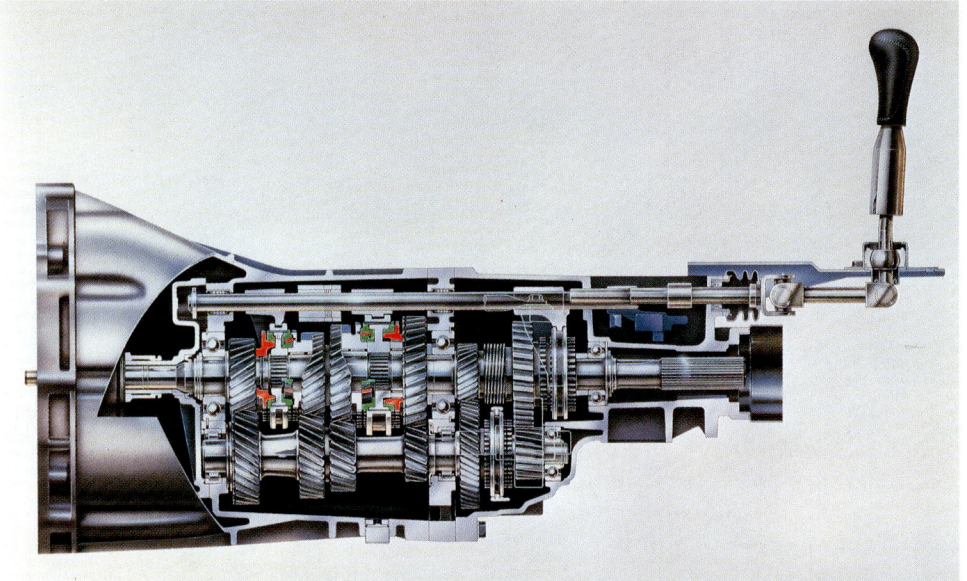

Cross-section of revised R30A five-speed manual gearbox shows remote lever linkage of support-rod type. Double cone synchronizers (below left) were deemed necessary for second and third gears to achieve the required change quality.

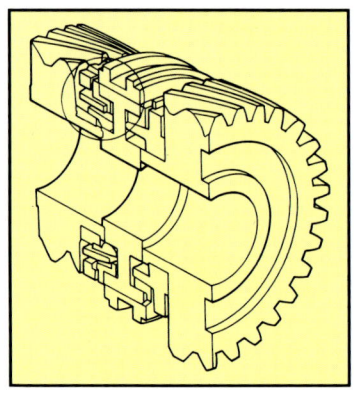

Automatic transmission is four-speed, with overdrive top brought into operation by a button on the selector lever. DUET electronic programme adjusts ignition to smooth shifts.

that the trend towards greater power outputs and higher engine rpm had increased the load on the gear synchronizers, which translates for the driver into a gearshift that needs a lot of effort. Calculations showed that the new 300ZX's R30A transmission with conventional synchromesh would have an unacceptably heavy change, particularly from second to third gear. The solution was to develop a high-capacity, double-cone synchronizer. This system separates the conventional synchro cone from the gear itself so that it can move along the shaft and friction torque for synchronizing the gears can be generated simultaneously on both its inner and outer surfaces.

Double-cone synchronizers are used only on second and third gears, as these are the most frequent shifts and the effort required for the changes to and from fourth and fifth was found to be low enough with the conventional synchro. (There was in any case no room to fit the double-cone type on the countershaft for fifth gear.) Some resistance when changing into first was thought desirable to warn against mis-shifts.

The transmission engineers discovered that the gearlever itself played a major part in shift quality. Convention says that a sports car gearlever should be short and need small movements. It was also important to eliminate vibration through the linkage. What was done here was to devise a remote linkage and support the

ANALYSIS

gearlever pivot with a solid rod – which required a slight increase in the height of the transmission tunnel inside the car. This enabled the lever to be placed in an optimum position and sit vertically rather than be angled, so that shifts are all in a horizontal plane.

Gearchange quality does not end with the gearbox, for the clutch action must be complementary. Both versions have hydraulic actuation, but the larger diameter clutch of the Turbo with its higher clamping load turned out to require 40lb pedal pressure and that was reckoned to be too heavy: 'It would ruin your shoes!,' says Toshimasa Doi. Consequently the Turbo has vacuum assistance from a device like a brake servo. It reduces the pedal effort to under 30lb, only a little more than the normally aspirated car's.

Though it may seem a contradiction of the considerable efforts Nissan expended on finding a formula for a true sports car, automatic transmission was part of the plan for the new 300ZX from the start. Some customers would demand it; in some markets, like Japan, the ratio of automatic to manual was expected to be more than 50%.

Two versions of the RE4R four-speed automatic are produced for the 300ZX, that used in the Turbo being the same as fitted to the Infiniti Q45. Both have convertor lock-up for greater efficiency but the Turbo has a more sophisticated electronic control system. Appropriately called DUET, this links engine and transmission electronics so that the ECCS can momentarily retard the ignition to lower engine torque and smooth an up-shift.

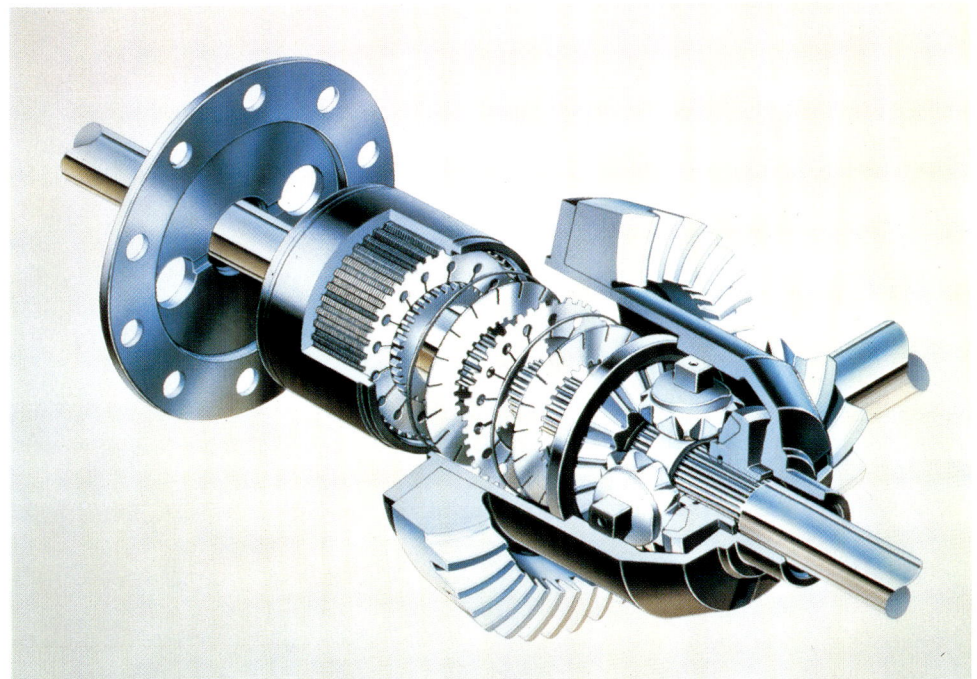

Viscous coupling limited-slip differential uses shear-effect of high-viscosity silicon oil against perforated plates to detect differences of speed between wheels and transfer torque.

The high ratio top gear of the automatic is engaged by a press-button overdrive switch built into the selector knob.

The final aspect of the driveline worthy of note is the limited-slip differential. Such devices are standard fitting on the more exotic powerful sports cars and, of course, for competition cars. The new 300ZX, like a special edition of its predecessor, is unusual in using a viscous coupling instead of some kind of mechanical limited-slip device.

The viscous coupling, in which two sets of perforated plates rotate in high viscosity silicon oil that 'stiffens' when there is a difference in speed of rotation from one side to the other, is an integral part of many of today's four-wheel drive systems. Motor industry engineers who are convinced about the vc's efficacy as a centre differential for four-wheel drive are divided over its value as an axle limited-slip differential. Ford of Europe use one at the rear in the Sierra and Scorpio 4X4s, but others say that the speed of operation is too slow to compensate for wheelspin and sharpen handling. Nissan disagree, pointing to the vc's progressive action, which aids stability and traction so smoothly that the driver hardly notices its good work.

Stiffening the structure

One element of the sports cars of old was that, compared with contemporary saloons, they were lightweight. That's no longer true even for small sports cars like the Mazda MX-5 and the Lotus Elan, and certainly not so with a car that has the 300ZX's level of equipment.

At NTC, the challenge for the new Z was to avoid an increase in weight – but at the same time to increase the bodyshell's rigidity significantly. Radical construction methods were quickly dismissed in the planning process. Unlike a Lotus, a BMW Z1, or even a Honda NS-X, this was to be a high volume sports car to be made in a conventional mass-production factory which was set up to produce welded steel unitary body/chassis.

A very rigid structure was important not only for a feeling of solidity and the reduction of shakes, rattles and vibrations, but also to give a firm basis for the new multi-link suspension. There would be little point in having a complex suspension set-up which required precise alignment of its various elements if the bodyshell itself was flexible.

The development of the shell was a job for the supercomputer, the use of which Nissan have developed even to give highly accurate predictions of crash deformation. These are not acceptable in lieu of actual crash tests, but are nevertheless very useful as they allow simulated barrier tests to be carried out before prototypes are built.

Compared with its predecessor, the new 300ZX turned out to have a 35% increase in bending rigidity and 20% in torsional rigidity. The T-bar version of the new car is better than the previous hardtop. The body is 55lb heavier than the old one, which was deemed acceptable.

ANALYSIS

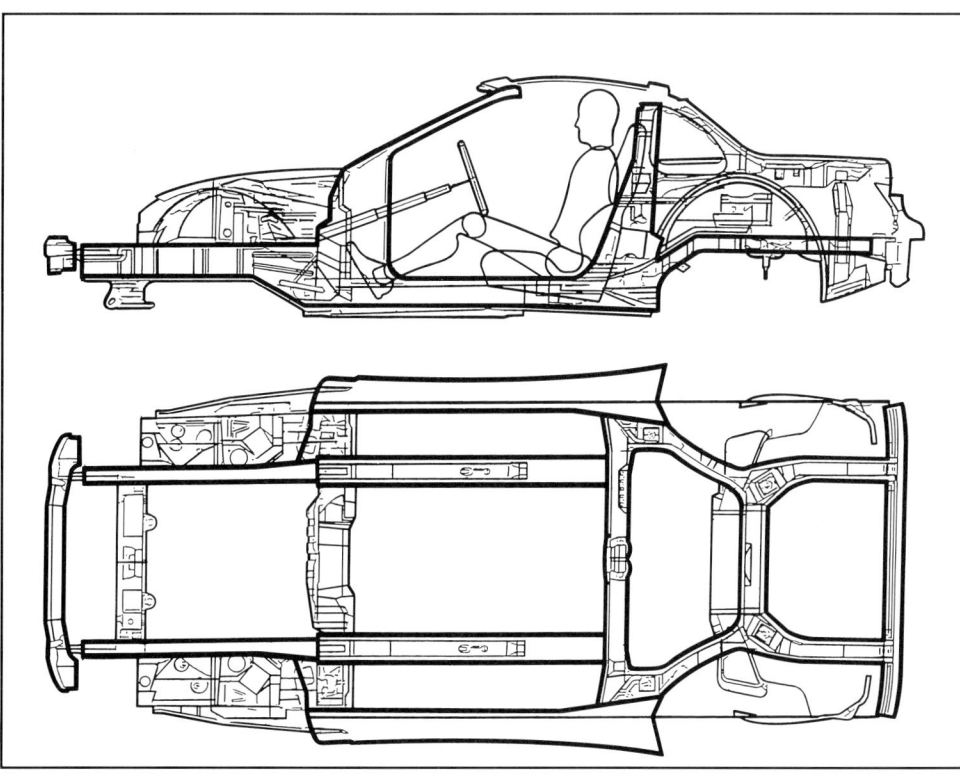

Side drawing of the underbody shows reinforced box-sections forming underfloor frame. Combined with front bulkhead, screen pillars, B-pillars and roof hoop, these produce an extra-strong 'safety zone' around the cockpit. Most of the shell is made from zinc-nickel plated Dura-Steel.

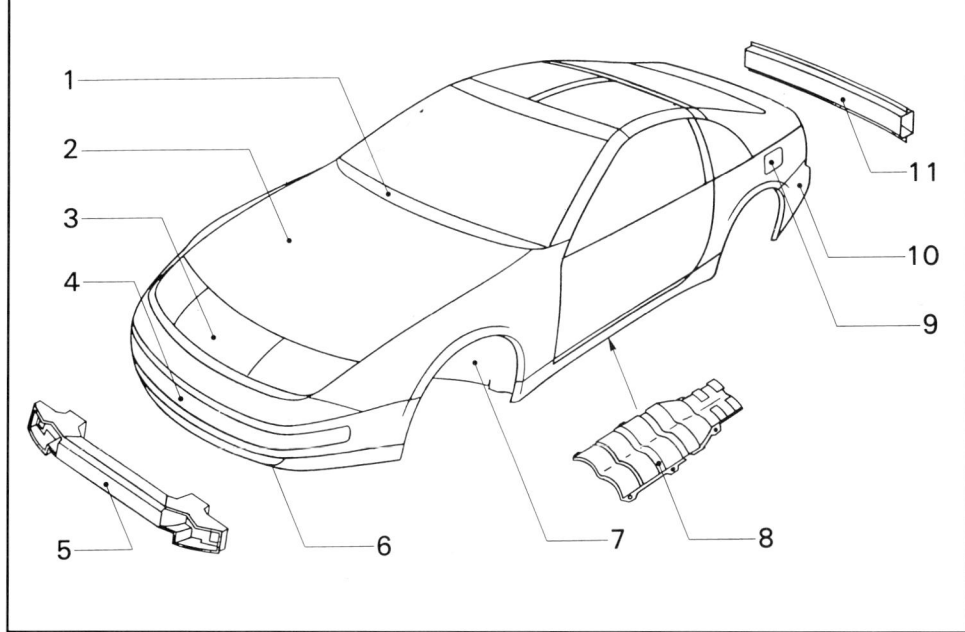

Use of aluminium and plastic, below – 1. cowl panel (polyphenylene oxide); 2. bonnet (aluminium); 3. front finisher panel (SMC); 4. bumper outer (glassfibre reinforced polyurethane); 5. front bumper armature (aluminium); 6. splash shields (polypropylene); 7. wing liner (polyethylene); 8. catalyst insulator (aluminium); 9. fuel filler lid (nylon); 10. bumper outer (polyurethane); 11. bumper armature (aluminium).

To achieve this strength and weight, they have used a combination of materials and some specific reinforcement. Continuous seam welding is used instead of (or rather, as well as) robot spot welding in some key areas, while others have reinforced box-sections which form a kind of supplementary underfloor frame. Aluminium and plastics have been used in some non-structural areas, notably the engine cover (aluminium) and the front and rear bumper shells (polyurethane), while high-tensile steel is used for the body reinforcements, the outer door skins and the front wings.

Dura Steel – zinc/nickel plated on both sides – is widely used for the outer body panels for good corrosion resistance. Panels which are most likely to be damaged in collisions are of modular design for easy replacement.

Apart from being 8in longer, the 2+2 structure differs from the two-seater in the position of the fuel tank, which is located behind rather than ahead of the rear axle line. The corresponding position of the fuel filler flap is an easy identification for the two models.

The door design is unusual in incorporating glass which is nearly flush, but does not have a full window frame. The window system is like the Audi 100's in that the glass is supported by studs running in tracks, rather than at its edges. The rear track sticks up from the trailing edge of the door, a substantial structure which in US models also carries the seat belt anchorage and so requires an additional latch mechanism at the top.

Suspension rethink

A car's structure does, of course, have a major influence on its road behaviour: its wheelbase and track, driveline arrangement, weight distribution, and the rigidity of the shell. But even with these factors near to ideal, these days it is no longer satisfactory to take a simple saloon car suspension system and expect it to provide the quality of roadholding and handling of a sports car. The role models for the new 300ZX are more sophisticated than that.

The suspension engineers at NTC were aware that the old ZX's industry-standard arrangement of MacPherson struts and semi-trailing arm suspension could not be developed to match their ambitions for the new car. They had reached the same conclusion in assessing the needs of other future rear-wheel drive cars – like the 200/240SX and the Infiniti Q45. So the programme which was to develop the new multi-link suspension was broader than just the new 300ZX. According to the manager of the No 1 chassis design department, Yuuichi Sanada, it involved no less than 600 engineers, 500 prototype vehicles and 6 million miles of testing.

Their broad aims were summarized thus: to improve the capabilities of the suspension – in other words, the car's roadholding; to maintain vehicle stability at all times by controlling toe-angle changes; and to achieve a flat ride by minimizing pitching motions during acceleration or deceleration. In the case of the 300ZX Turbo, the Infiniti Q45 and the Skyline GT-R, they added a fourth

Layout of the 300ZX multi-link front suspension. Lower wishbone is made up of transverse link with forward-facing tension rod. Upper arm is twisted forward to optimize wheel location and has an unusual third link to allow near-ideal geometry.

objective of further improving handling and stability by using electronic technology to achieve active toe control at the rear wheels; the Super HICAS rear-wheel steering system is described in detail on page 52.

They concluded that the double-wishbone (or A-arm) suspension of racing and sports cars could not, in its classic form, achieve Nissan's objectives and be accommodated within the 300ZX body. Painstaking further development eventually produced multi-link systems for both front and rear.

In a rear-wheel-drive car, the rear suspension is the major contributor to stability, while the front provides most to the handling performance. Chronologically, the development started with the rear suspension, but our 300ZX description will progress logically from front to rear.

The starting point for the front suspension was a double-wishbone layout. The first difficulty was that the engine position prevented the conventional upper link being of sufficient length to optimize camber change. The solution to that was to re-position the upper arm up above the wheel (Honda have done something similar with the Accord), where it could be as long as needed. Because this also increases the span between upper and lower links it provides increased alignment stiffness to the benefit of steering control and high speed and braking stability.

But the high upper arm means that the position of the outer pivot that determines the angle of the steering axis is also high and relatively distanced from the body, which would have the disadvantage of increasing the scrub radius. The answer to this was to add another link from the upper arm to a point on the ideal steering axis. This 'third link' has a bearing at the lower end which joins to the kingpin extension. Thus the upper arm is freed from the restrictions imposed by the steering axis, allowing optimum geometry. Furthermore, if the upper arm is twisted forward it can achieve both the small camber change with suspension stroke required for good straight-line stability and the increased camber with body roll desirable for control near the cornering limit. It also helps control nose-dive during braking.

The third link provides a convenient mounting for the coil spring/damper unit, leaving a space inside the hub which, coincidentally, allows the system to be applied to front- or four-wheel drive cars; the new Primera saloon uses a similar multi-link layout.

At the rear, Nissan's multi-link suspension differs in geometry, but not in principle, from that adopted by other makers who offer powerful rear-drive cars, notably BMW and Mercedes. Again, it is based on a double-wishbone layout, but has an extra lateral lower link. Properly designed double-wishbone systems can achieve a low roll centre and ideal wheel camber control, as well as minimizing tail squat when accelerating and tail lift under braking.

The Nissan scheme was shown in an earlier form back in 1985 on the original Mid-4 and CUE-X prototypes. Called DARS (for Diagonal A-arm Rear Suspension), it mounts the lower wishbone at an angle to the car's centreline. When roll or a

Multi-link rear suspension is shared with other rear-drive Nissans including the 200SX. It has a lower diagonally mounted wishbone with an additional transverse link. The two top links act independently, the rearmost forming a hoop through which the spring/shock absorber passes.

braking force is applied to it, the wishbone slides back against its bushings, providing a small degree of toe-in at the wheel to aid stability.

For the 300ZX, the two top links that replace the wishbone act independently. The intention here is to achieve consistent handling under deceleration. A car slows down either on the brakes, when the forces are applied through the tyres, or by engine braking, when the forces act at the centres of the wheels; the tendency for the rear wheels to toe-in is therefore different in the two cases. By carefully angling the two upper arms, they were able to equalize the effect in either braking condition.

Devising the geometry for these multi-link systems was a complicated business which required a great deal of analysis by the supercomputer. Not only did the apparently conflicting axes of the various links have to be calculated but also the distortion of the rubber bushes at the mountings, since their compliance is an important factor in the efficiency of the system.

Such sophisticated arrangements eliminate many compromises of simpler suspension systems, so that the springs, shock absorbers and stabilizer bars can be softer than is usual for a car of this type, resulting in improved ride comfort.

Style stoppers

Suspension designers are always keen to reduce unsprung weight but when the components involved – the wheels and brakes – have to sustain and stop a 150mph car there is a limit to how far they can be lightened.

So reducing the weight of each front brake caliper by 4.4lb while also increasing their efficiency compared with the previous 300ZX was quite an achievement. NTC engineers devised a new disc brake system for the latest model which features aluminium calipers which are light but rigid and operate

300ZX

on substantial ventilated rotors. The front calipers are of the opposed four-piston type – derived from racing technology.

Electronic anti-lock braking is a standard fitment. As with all such systems, the main advantage is not so much in reducing stopping distances in a straight line as allowing steering control to be maintained while braking. Some car manufacturers believe that it is desirable to have the brake pedal kick back as a warning to the driver when ABS is operating; Nissan don't and have included a special device in their system to reduce kick back.

The style of the 300ZX's cast aluminium wheels is directly related to the braking system, for it was evident that they must provide for brake cooling. A chosen design has five narrow spokes and is unidirectional to encourage airflow between them. This open style meant that the brakes themselves would be partly exposed so it was decided to make a feature of them. The design department was brought in to style the caliper castings, including the Nissan name in raised lettering. The 300ZX is in good company here – Porsche's formidable 959 shows off its brakes in similar fashion!

Wheel rim diameter is 16in, width 7.5in (8.5in at the rear on the Turbo), allowing the fitment of the latest ultra-low profile tyres. These are 225/50ZR16 Bridgestone, Dunlop or Michelin, depending on the market. The Turbo's wider rears are 245/45ZR16, except in Japan where, for some unaccountable reason, domestic manufacturers are not allowed to fit 45-profile tyres.

A turn for the better

It is no longer sissy for a sports car to have power steering, even if some of the more exotic mid- and rear-engined cars still get away without it. But with a good 50% of 1½ tons over the front wheels and tyres that are 8in wide, driving a

Electronic anti-lock braking system, below left, has speed sensors at each wheel connected to microprocessor at the back of the car which modulates brake operation if the onset of wheel lock is detected. Heat transfer in caliper and disc was studied in computer simulation, below, to arrive at optimum size and weight.

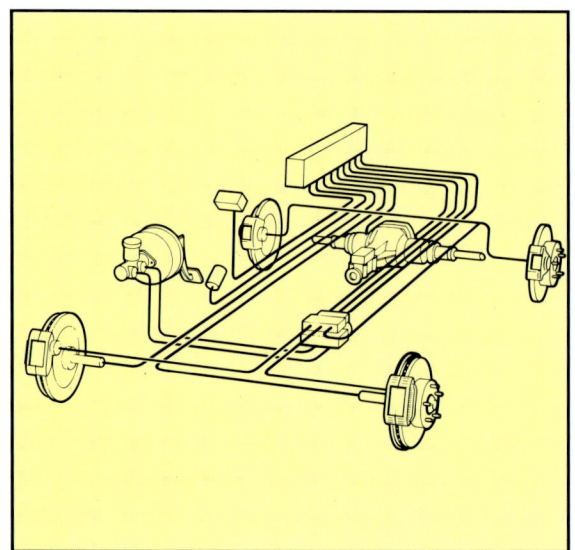
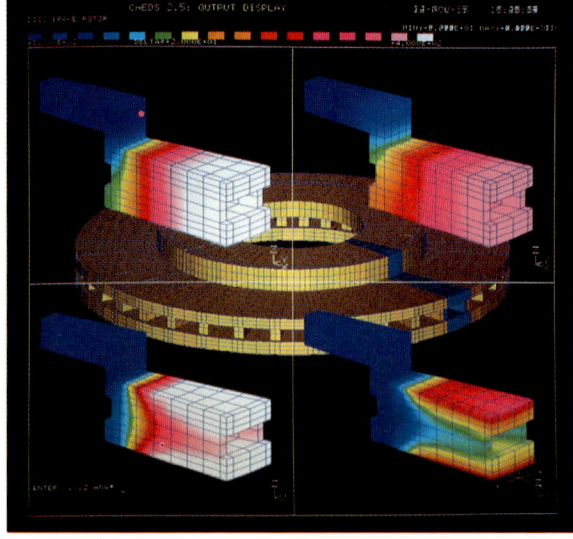

Distinctive cast alloy wheels, right, are attractive and functional, designed to cool exposed brake calipers.

300ZX without power assistance would be mighty heavy work.

The term power steering covers a multitude of systems. Some are too light, which though fine for parking, can mean that they transmit too little information at higher speeds. Others do not provide enough assistance, so the car seems reluctant to turn. The best aspects of both can be combined by decreasing assistance with engine revs or as the vehicle speed rises. This is achieved by restricting the flow of fluid through a control valve – an orifice – in the hydraulic system that provides the assistance. However, in its simpler forms, this kind of power steering can be starved of fluid during a series of steering manoeuvres, which leads to inconsistent response.

After studying existing systems, Nissan engineers developed one which was vehicle speed-sensitive but novel in some important respects. They installed two variable-orifice valves in sequence, rather in the way of wiring two batteries in series, and placed a variable drain valve between them. At low speeds the drain valve is closed and maximum assistance is provided through both open orifices. As the car's speed rises, an electronic impulse opens the drain valve, which diverts the fluid from the first orifice, bypassing the second and thus reducing the pressure and the assistance. A microprocessor calculates the amount of steering effort required according to the car's speed and gradually reduces the amount of assistance as it goes faster.

The actual steering gear system is rack and pinion and its overall ratio is 'quick' at 2.5 turns lock-to-lock for the US Turbo, though other models have a slightly lower ratio, needing 2.7 turns.

The 300ZX Turbo has one extra technical feature of which the engineers are especially proud: Super HICAS. Other Japanese manufacturers offer four-wheel steering and in the case of Honda and Mazda it is two-phase, assisting low-speed manoeuvres as well as enhancing high-speed stability. Super HICAS is also two-phase, but of more subtle character. It is not arranged to make it easier to squeeze into parking spaces. The rear-wheel steering, which never exceeds plus or minus 1 degree, is purely designed to improve the car's response in medium and high-speed swerves.

The rear-wheel steering system, which is integrated with the multi-link suspension and the front-wheel steering, is electro-hydraulic. It operates like this: electronic sensors detect the car's speed, steering angle and steering wheel movement, and if they exceed predetermined values, the computer directs a hydraulic actuator at the rear axle to steer the rear wheels via the rearmost lower suspension links. In normal driving the movement is rarely more than 0.4 degree.

But, unlike other 4WS systems which, at speed, steer the rear wheels in the same sense as the front ones, Super HICAS first introduces a twitch of counter-steer before settling with all four wheels pointing in the same direction. The degree or suddenness of this touch of opposite lock is reduced as the speed rises.

Super HICAS automatically produces a precise form of the rally driver's technique of flicking the steering to the outside of a corner before turning into it. The result for the 300ZX is very sharp 'turn-in', with better stability through the classic lane-change manoeuvre which reproduces emergency evasive action at speed. An ordinary car tends to swing its tail in such circumstances, but 4WS allows the front and rear tyres to develop their slip angles simultaneously to the benefit of handling.

If it is so good and they are so pleased with it, why doesn't Nissan fit Super HICAS to the normally aspirated 300ZX as well? The answer is about economics, but NTC's testers say that the real benefits of the rear-steer become apparent at over 120mph and that they are happy with the handling of the regular car without it. The 300ZX Turbo, with its considerably higher speed potential, needed Super HICAS if it was to achieve the ambitious handling and stability standards they had set themselves.

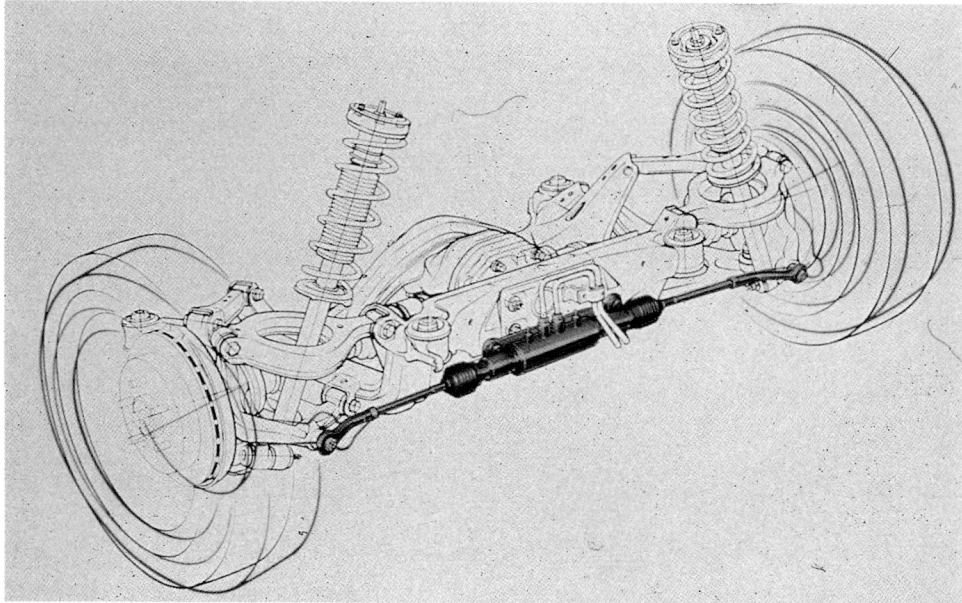

Rear-wheel steering is operated by hydraulic actuator mounted behind the differential. Diagram above right shows elements of the system and its actuation. Nissan's claimed advantages of Super HICAS over two-wheel steering and other forms of four-wheel steering are presented in the diagram, right, showing car behaviour in a high-speed lane change.

ANALYSIS

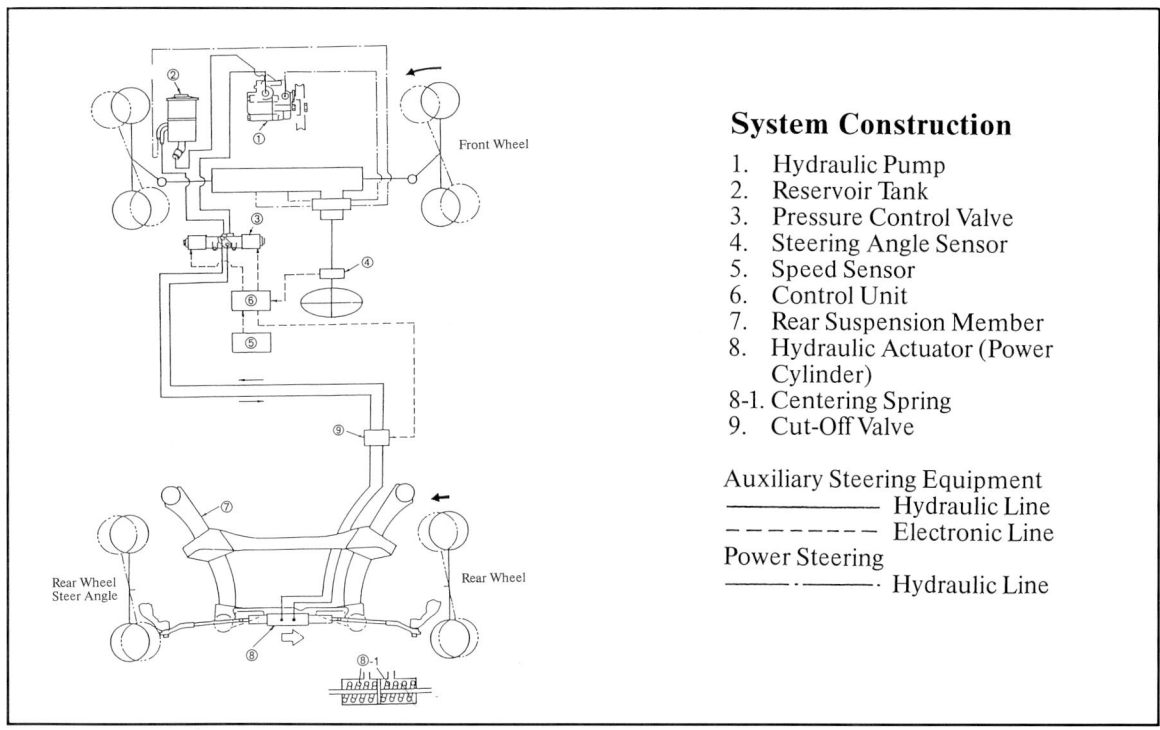

System Construction

1. Hydraulic Pump
2. Reservoir Tank
3. Pressure Control Valve
4. Steering Angle Sensor
5. Speed Sensor
6. Control Unit
7. Rear Suspension Member
8. Hydraulic Actuator (Power Cylinder)
8-1. Centering Spring
9. Cut-Off Valve

Auxiliary Steering Equipment
——————— Hydraulic Line
– – – – – – – Electronic Line
Power Steering
—·—·—·— Hydraulic Line

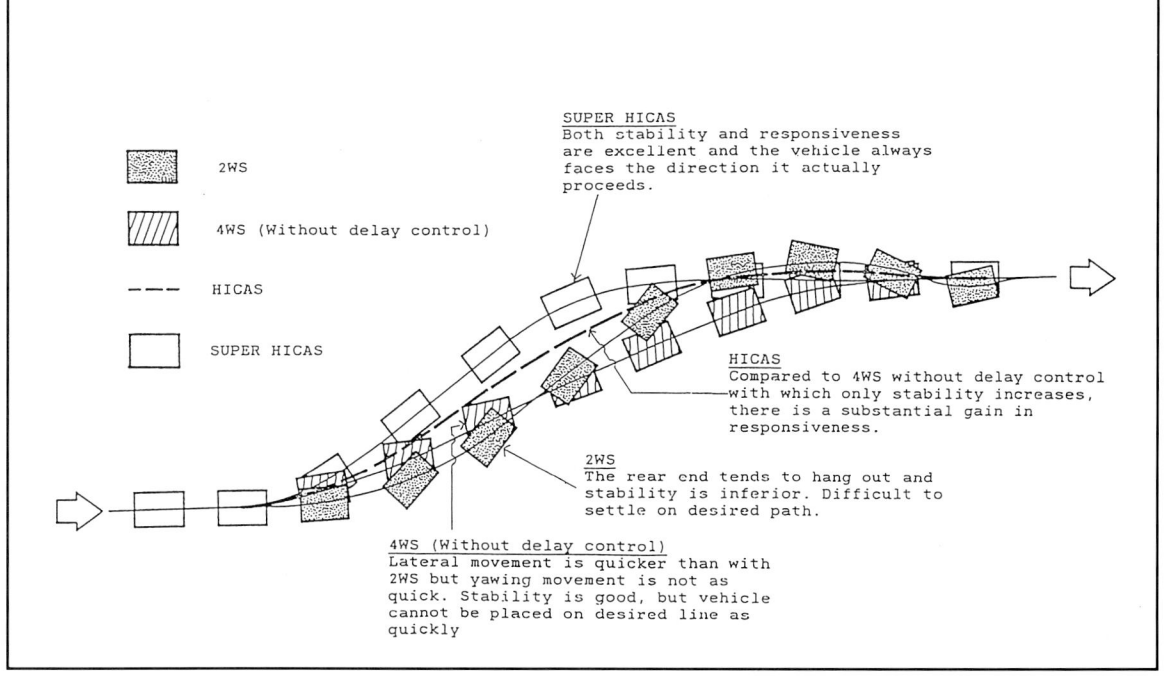

SUPER HICAS
Both stability and responsiveness are excellent and the vehicle always faces the direction it actually proceeds.

HICAS
Compared to 4WS without delay control with which only stability increases, there is a substantial gain in responsiveness.

2WS
The rear end tends to hang out and stability is inferior. Difficult to settle on desired path.

4WS (Without delay control)
Lateral movement is quicker than with 2WS but yawing movement is not as quick. Stability is good, but vehicle cannot be placed on desired line as quickly

Specifications

300ZX

Engine (normally aspirated, Type VG30DE)
V6, 2,960cc (87mm X 83mm), iron block, aluminium heads, belt-driven double overhead camshafts per bank, 24 valves, electronic variable valve timing, direct ignition (individual coil per plug), electronic sequential multi-point port fuel injection. Three-way catalytic convertor with electronic feedback air-fuel ratio control. Exhaust gas recirculation. Compression ratio 10.5:1.
Maximum power 222bhp at 6,400rpm.
Maximum torque 198lb/ft at 4,800rpm.

Transmission
Five-speed manual, all-synchromesh.
Ratios (mph per 1,000rpm):
1st 3.21 (5.5)
2nd 1.93 (9.1)
3rd 1.30 (13.5)
4th 1.00 (17.6)
5th 0.75 (23.4)

Four-speed automatic, electronic control, lock-up torque convertor.
Ratios:
1st 2.79
2nd 1.55
3rd 1.00
4th 0.69

Final-drive ratio: 4.083.
Viscous coupling limited-slip differential.

Suspension
Front: Independent, multi-link, coil springs, telescopic shock absorbers, anti-roll bar.
Rear: Independent, multi-link, coil springs, telescopic shock absorbers, anti-roll bar.

Steering
Power-assisted rack and pinion, electronically speed-variable assistance. Ratio 16.8:1. 2.7 turns from lock to lock. 34.1ft turning circle (two-seater), 35.4ft (2+2).

Brakes
Front: 11.0in ventilated disc, dual caliper, four-piston.
Rear: 11.7in ventilated discs, dual caliper, two-piston.
Electronic anti-lock braking system.

Wheels
7.5J, 16in diameter cast aluminium alloy, with 225/50VR16 tyres.

Fuel tank: 15.8 Imp gal/18.7 US gal/72 litres.
Kerb weight: 3,219lb (two-seater), 3,313lb (2+2).
Weight distribution (F/R): 55:45 (two-seater), 53:47 (2+2).

300ZX TURBO

Engine (Type VG30DETT)
V6, 2,960cc (87mm X 83mm), iron block, aluminium heads, belt-driven double overhead camshafts per bank, 24 valves, electronic variable valve timing, direct ignition (individual coil per plug), electronic sequential multi-point port fuel injection. Two Garrett T2/2.5 turbochargers with air-to-air intercoolers. Three-way catalytic convertor with electronic feedback air-fuel ratio control. Exhaust gas recirculation. Compression ratio: 8.5:1.

US specification:
Manual – maximum power 300bhp (SAE net) at 6,400rpm, maximum torque 283lb/ft at 3,600rpm.
Automatic – maximum power 280bhp (SAE net) at 6,400rpm, maximum torque 283lb/ft at 3,600rpm.

European specification:
Maximum power 280PS at 6,400rpm. Maximum torque 275lb/ft at 3,600rpm.

Transmission
Five-speed manual, all-synchromesh.

Ratios:
1st 3.21
2nd 1.93
3rd 1.30
4th 1.00
5th 0.75

Four-speed automatic, electronically controlled, lock-up torque convertor.
Ratios:
1st 2.78
2nd 1.54
3rd 1.00
4th 0.69

Final-drive ratio: 4.083:1 (US), 3.69:1 (Europe). Viscous coupling limited-slip differential. Vacuum-assisted clutch.

Suspension
Front: Independent, multi-link, coil springs, telescopic shock absorbers, anti-roll bar.
Rear: Independent, multi-link, coil springs, telescopic shock absorbers, anti-roll bar.

Steering
Power-assisted rack and pinion, electronically speed-variable assistance. Ratio 14.8:1 (US), 16.8:1 (Europe).
Turns lock to lock: 2.5 (US), 2.7 (Europe).
Turning circle: 34.1ft (two-seater), 36.7ft (2+2).
Super HICAS rear-wheel steering system with phase-reversal control.

Brakes
Front: 11.0in ventilated disc, dual caliper, four-piston.
Rear: 11.7in ventilated discs, dual caliper, two-piston.
Vacuum assist. Electronic anti-lock braking system.

Wheels
Front: 7.5J, 16in diameter cast aluminium alloy, with 225/50ZR16 tyres.
Rear: 8.5J, 16in diameter cast aluminium alloy, with
245/45ZR16 tyres.

Fuel tank: 15.8 Imp gal/ 18.7 US gal/ 72 litres.

Kerb weight: 3,414lb (two-seater), 3,495lb (2+2 manual), 3,516lb (2+2 automatic).

Weight distribution (F/R): 55:45 (two-seater), 53:47 (2+2).

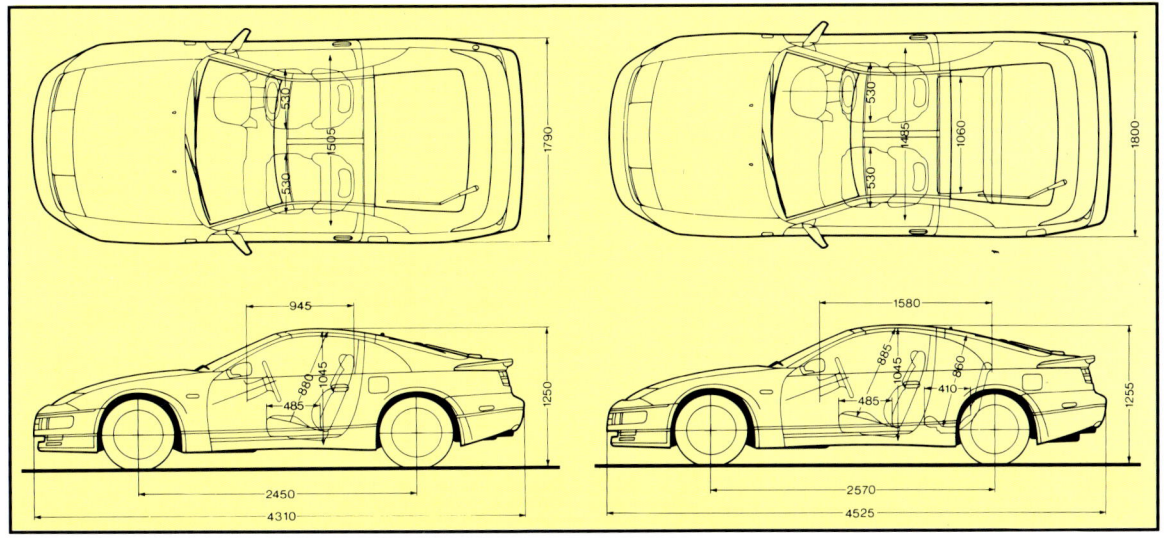

Dimensions of 300ZX two-seater, left, and 2+2, right, in millimetres. Track measurements are 1496mm and 1534mm (normally aspirated rear), 1554mm Turbo rear.

The making of the 300ZX

A visit to Hiratsuka, home of the Z-car, to see how the new model is built and tested

Nissan Shatai's plant in Hiratsuka City is not the kind of showpiece production facility that is used to demonstrate the latest in Japanese technology to VIP visitors. In fact, it is rather comforting in its middle-tech ordinariness.

The Hiratsuka factory has robotized welding machinery to ensure consistent strength and accuracy, but no more than in the average European or US factory of comparable size. Mostly, its results depend on the care and dedication of the people who work on the assembly line. And evidently they are proud to make the Nissan Z-car. Signs all around welcome visitors to the birthplace of the Fairlady Z, 'Number 1 sports car of the world'. They have made 1.3 million of them since 1969.

Nissan Shatai is only 60% owned by Nissan Motor and is an industrial group in its own right, with manufacturing, real-estate, leisure goods, car sales and maintenance businesses as well as vehicle production for Nissan. Apart from the Z, the Hiratsuka plant builds the Prairie/Axxess and Bluebird wagons, vans, and a 4wd pickup truck.

Nissan Shatai produce all the pressings for the 300ZX's unitary body structure, including the aluminium bonnet, and also mould the main plastic structures, including the bumper casings and the instrument panel. The main body framing is performed automatically using the one-jig assembly method but there is quite a lot of hand welding, particularly where seam welds are specified for added strength.

There is no room at Hiratsuka for a test track, so each car has an elaborate rolling-road test at the end of the final assembly line using interactive electronics to check all the car's systems.

All 300ZX Turbos destined for Europe go from there to a special high-speed dynamometer where a driver puts them through another 50-minute cycle which involves a further and even more thorough test of engine and transmission. Speeds, temperatures, pressures and exhaust emissions are monitored in the control booth and recorded on a computer printout. Each car is run to and held at its maximum speed; though the Turbo is in theory limited to 250km/hr (155mph) they do not seem to be too concerned about the occasional example that attains 165...

There is only one of these high-speed dynos at Hiratsuka and initially it was being used to test about 100 cars a month. The man in charge of it is probably the only person in Nissan who hopes that the 300ZX does not become too popular in Europe because his department could not cope!

Roof, floor, bulkheads and side panels are welded automatically on a single jig, but seam welding to add strength in key areas is carried out by hand. There is an evident pride in working on the ZX at Nissan Shatai.

New painting procedures (left) improve the smoothness of finish by laser surface-treatment of the steel and using robot sprayers that constantly maintain an equal distance from the car body.

At the end of the production line each 300ZX goes through an extensive series of checks on a rolling road dynamometer (right). The car's electrical system is hooked up to a computer monitoring system and the operator goes through a check sequence.

Much of the final assembly process (left) is carried out with the car suspended overhead. Complex mechanical and electrical items – including the multi-link suspension – are put together off-line as sub-assemblies.

Mindful of hard use on the autobahn, Nissan Shatai put all 300ZX Turbos for the European market through an additional test regime (right) on this high-speed dynamometer. It is a 50-minute running cycle, including a spell at maximum speed.

The American road – Car and Driver's long-term test 300ZX Turbo two-seater during a winter work-out in Michigan.

TESTED

Balanced assessment

Ray Hutton tests the 300ZX variants on road and track, in Britain, Japan and the USA

Cars have changed a lot in two decades and standard-setting sports cars more than most. I had a Datsun 240Z in 1972 and loved every mile in it. Having learnt something about fast cars in my old Triumph TR3 with its dodgy handling, bone-jarring ride and draughty sidescreens, and dallied with MGBs and TR6s in my early days as a motoring writer, the Z seemed to me the epitome of the civilized modern sports car.

And so it was, at the time. Being designed as a fixed-head coupe, the 240Z had a solid feel that the open two-seaters all lacked. It had the style of the class above – the Jaguar E-types and the Porsches – rather than looking like a cut-down saloon or an old-fashioned roadster weatherproofed with a crude plastic hardtop.

As the 1970s progressed, other manufacturers followed the Z's theme, though British Leyland lost interest and the variety of sports cars available from volume manufacturers reduced. But the Datsun Z-car did not improve with age. I tried most of the variants through to the 280 and 300ZX. In 1988, on a visit to Detroit, I drove the 300ZX Turbo with the final restyling by Nissan's San Diego design studio. My notes say: 'Despite a neat facelift and all the equipment that anyone could ask for, this car is beginning to look and feel very old'.

On a return trip the following year my colleagues at *Car and Driver* were talking very enthusiastically about the new 300ZX which had been launched at the 1989 Chicago Auto Show. 'Forget about the old Zee,' they told me. 'They have done a really good job with the new one.' Larry Griffin, writing in the March 1989 *Car and Driver* about a preview drive at Nissan's Tochigi proving ground, said: 'A good car tells you it's on the right track as soon as you drive away. The new 300ZX told us within 50 feet. Everything felt hooked up, ready to run and gun...'

When my chance came to drive it, I knew what Larry meant. The low, wide, slant-eyed 300ZX is alluring. It invites you to get in and take a ride, and once behind the wheel, the cockpit feels so right that you *expect* the dynamics to match the visual appeal. They do.

This was a normally aspirated two-seater in bright pearlescent yellow. We felt at home, the two of us, that summer's day on the quiet roads of northern Michigan. The 300ZX turned out to be one of those cars which inspired the confidence to drive fast after only a short time behind the wheel. The controls worked with a smooth precision. Bumps and broken road surfaces did not deflect its course. And the engine was so sweet and smooth that it was a pleasure to run it up to its 7,000rpm red line.

High-speed action for a European-specification 300ZX. Cars for Europe are Turbo 2+2 only; US market Turbo is only two-seater.

300ZX

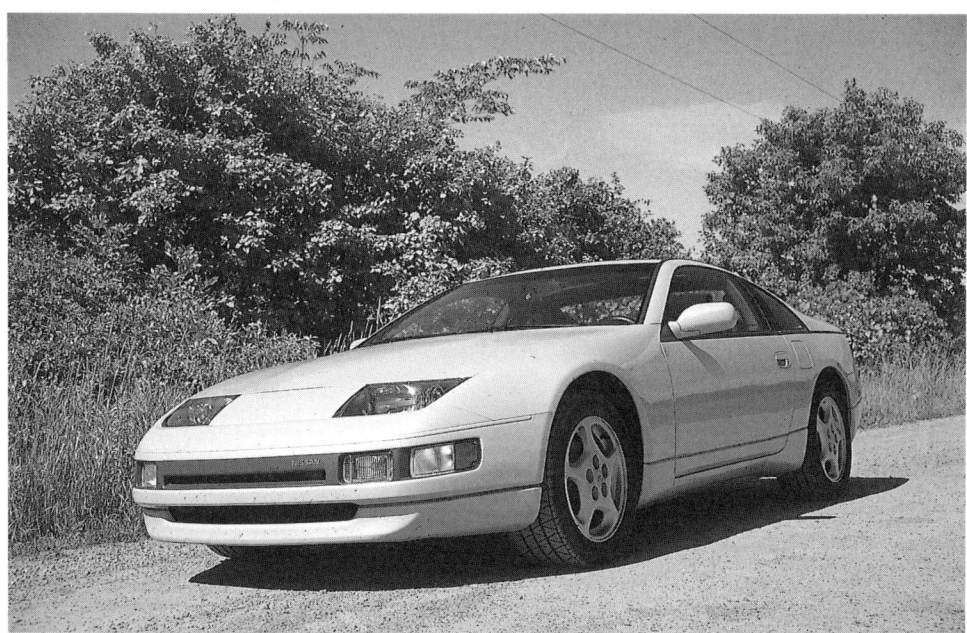

Normally aspirated 300ZX (this page) has shallower front air dam and lacks the tail spoiler of the Turbo opposite. Though there is 8.5in between them, the two-seater and 2+2 are hard to tell apart. A quick identification point is the fuel filler position; two-seaters have the filler flap ahead of the rear wheel, 2+2 location is behind the wheelarch.

TESTED

Though Porsche fans rave about the 911, it is the front-engined 944 and 928 that set the handling standards. The 944, in particular, has poise – superb balance that makes it both enjoyable and predictable to drive fast. My conclusion from that first drive in the new 300ZX was that it sat between the 944 and 928. In terms of bulk – width and weight – it matches the latter and the curved, enclosing 'cockpit', with its neat, business-like instrument binnacle, is a development of the 928's. Performance, with the 222bhp normally aspirated engine, was in the 944 class. More important, so was its road behaviour – taut, with very little body roll, dip or squat; lots of grip from Michelin Sport XGTV tyres; superbly accurate steering with unobtrusive power assistance; neutral handling just edging towards understeer. It had that subtle, hard-to-achieve thing – balance.

It is a motoring writer's cliche that any car which is capable of effortless fast cornering *and* handles safely needs more power. Certainly, several who tested the first 300ZX remarked that good as this one was, the Turbo version was sure to be better. When it arrived that autumn, their reports confirmed that view. I had a hunch that the normally aspirated 300ZX would be the nicer for everyday motoring. In any case, with a maximum speed of 143mph and 0–60mph acceleration well under 7sec, it was no slouch – faster than a regular 944 and not much slower than a Chevrolet Corvette Z51.

My first opportunity to feel the difference that two turbochargers can make was in Japan, at Tochigi, in the autumn of 1989. It was at a preview of the

300ZX

European-specification 300ZX – which is exclusively Turbo 2+2. First experience was on the banked high-speed oval, where the car ran up to an indicated maximum of 260km/hr (160mph – though the true speed was probably somewhat lower). That this seemed unremarkable was in itself impressive. The engine, running at over 6,500rpm, was uncomplaining. The car felt rock-steady. And the loudest sound was the rush of the wind.

Later, on the tricky Tochigi country road course (see page 76) the Turbo's mighty power was more obvious. On the gentler curves it showed that same good balance, and it hung on impressively through tighter corners from a very eager turn-in (aided by Super HICAS) to an early bootful of throttle on the exit. That said, cresting the bigger mid-corner bumps with engine well wound up made one aware that here was a weighty car that might, at the very limit, become quite a handful.

Only a few weeks after driving the European 2+2 in Japan, I was able to spend a week with a US-specification Turbo two-seater loaned to *Car and Driver* for long-term evaluation. Comforted by a radar detector, I was able to confirm the arrow-straight stability at high speed on the highway. Off-ramps demonstrated the almost abrupt turn-in – and the care that needs to be taken with the throttle on slippery surfaces. There is power aplenty from low revs, but at 2,700rpm, when the turbo boost has built up, it is take-off time; this then becomes a seriously fast car.

The power transition is so smooth, and corners are negotiated with so little effort, that it is all-too easy to find oneself going a lot faster than anticipated. In the wet, or in ice and snow, such as I encountered in Illinois in February, the 300ZX needs respect. *Car and Driver* had found that the standard Michelin MXX tyres were unsuitable for a Mid-West winter and, after some experiment, fitted Goodrich Comp T/A VR4 all-weather rubber. These tyres are both grippy and progressive but could not eliminate some wheel-bounce when making a fast take-off on a slick surface.

I concluded that the Turbo and normally aspirated 300ZXs, though virtually identical to look at and travel in, are cars of rather different driving character. Where the regular car is light and easy to drive fast, the Turbo requires more effort and is more of an expert's car. The clutch is heavier, despite its servo. Though some will tell you that the turbochargers have no lag, it is not true. There is a very definite point at which boost starts to be delivered, but the transition is remarkably smooth – and, of course, the engine has plenty of punch without the extra charge. The result of this is that the driver of a manual-gearbox car has to pay attention to get the best out of the Turbo. It will go from 0–60mph in a Porsche-matching 5.5sec, but driven lazily it can be blown off at the traffic lights by lesser cars, including a normally aspirated 300ZX...

The US Turbo has notably sharper response, thanks to quicker steering (2.5 instead of 2.7 turns lock-to-lock) and Super HICAS. But it is less sporting in the way it sounds – the Turbo's complicated exhaust tracts dull the lovely growl of the normally aspirated V6 at high revs.

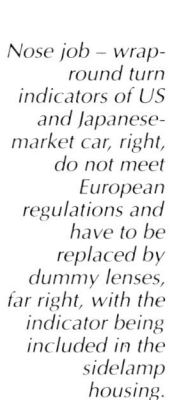

Nose job – wrap-round turn indicators of US and Japanese-market car, right, do not meet European regulations and have to be replaced by dummy lenses, far right, with the indicator being included in the sidelamp housing.

Tail-gate is a clamshell structure and when open leaves a curious-looking section of underbody exposed. Rear visibility and access to the luggage compartment are not the car's strongest points.

Rear aspect of the 300ZX is purposely tail-up, to give a racing-type glimpse of the mechanical elements. Rear and brake lamps, reflectors and reversing lights shine through a single-shade panel.

Glass roof panels are well-located and easy to unlatch and remove (they can also be locked in place for added security). With tops off and windows down, airflow is uncomfortable at speed.

Massive doors have a substantial rear pillar which, for US models, carries safety belt assembly and therefore also has an additional top latch. Flush side windows are supported by a frame inside the door and a surface guide on the rear pillar which is left exposed when the window is down.

Angle of the enormous windscreen is the most extreme of any volume-production car, but achieved without distortion. Continuous curvature through the cabin area is a distinctive styling feature.

TESTED

US and European 300ZX Turbos are different in ways apart from accommodation. In the past, a Japanese firm trying to tailor a sports model for specific markets would give a European car sharper responses and stiffer suspension and make the US version softer and more saloon-like. Nissan's research suggested that it should be the other way round. Perhaps because the American enthusiast magazines place such emphasis on lateral acceleration measurements, or just because the popular Corvette has race-track suspension, they reckon that US sports car customers today value quick response above all else. Hence, for the US, the turbocharged engine is available only in the two-seater body, it has two-position shock absorbers (normal settings are 20% stiffer than the normally aspirated car), quicker steering, and the electronics are calibrated to provide more eager operation of Super HICAS.

They may have taken these things a bit too far. I note that the 'sport' damper setting of the Turbo is too hard even for the keen testers at *Car and Driver*; they love their Corvettes but leave the 300ZX suspension switch at 'touring'. European and Japanese market cars are a little softer than that, but their ride would still be classified on the hard side; subjectively, harder than a regular Porsche 944 or 928S4.

Nissan's own test drivers admit that the 2+2, with its longer wheelbase (101.2in against 96.5) and more even weight distribution, is the more stable and better balanced of the two versions, while the two-seater is ultimately more agile and responsive, but they say that the difference is not great. In any case, the emphasis in developing the European version was towards high-speed stability – with unlimited autobahn driving uppermost in their minds.

Testing cars all over the world can be misleading. I had been impressed by the capabilities 300ZXs had shown on varied roads in the eastern United States, but it was important for me to try it in England, under more familiar conditions.

An obvious first observation was that a car that is an inch under six foot wide feels much bigger on British country lanes than on the wider roads of America, and that can inhibit fast, safe driving. Noise from the Michelin MXX tyres seemed more obtrusive than it had been in the US. On the plus side was the car's impressive stability when running at speed over some of the broken and uneven surfaces that have become a regrettable feature of much of the British road network.

I drove a Porsche 944 over a 30-mile road circuit in Northamptonshire and immediately afterwards followed the same route in a 300ZX, driving both cars fast but with what I judged to be the same margin of safety. The Nissan was considerably quicker – as I had expected – but it also gave this driver more confidence. Where the 944 steering feeds back every road imperfection and every camber change as a slight movement of the steering wheel, the ZX rode across them all, not only precisely on course, but also without transmitting the extent of its task. Richard Bremner of *Car* magazine also noted this in a comparison with a 944 Turbo and felt that it counted against the 300ZX. He wrote: 'In cold terms you cannot say that the Nissan doesn't go, grip, handle and

Inside story – main picture shows European specification 300ZX Turbo with left-hand drive, manual transmission and optional leather seating. Note cruise controls on the steering wheel centre, and headlamp height adjuster alongide mirror joystick on centre console. Automatic right-hand drive version, above, has regular cloth trim and automatic air conditioning. The Turbo below shows the compact disc player that is standard for the UK market.

manoeuvre as well as the Porsche. The difference is that it doesn't tell you how cleverly it's doing it. There's simply not enough drama in its excellence.'

In America, *Automobile* magazine published a similar comparison test at the time of the 300ZX Turbo introduction, which, symbolically, coincided with Porsche's withdrawal of the 944 Turbo from the US market. They noted that both cars produced 100bhp per litre, had similar power-to-weight ratios, ran on the same size tyres and recorded similar acceleration figures. On a race track they found the cars so closely matched that there was hardly anything to choose between them, but the testers agreed that the Nissan had the more forgiving handling. On the road its ride was more comfortable and its engine was quieter.

Over at *Car and Driver* they had really put their heads in the dragon's mouth: a wheel-to-wheel test of the 300ZX and the Chevrolet Corvette. This was a thorough investigation, taking in race track and road assessments and performance measurement at Chrysler's proving ground. The contenders were the 300ZX Turbo, 3 litres, 300bhp, 3,500lb and the Corvette Z51, 5.7 litres, 250bhp, 3,380lb. At the track – Grattan Raceway in Michigan – the Corvette showed best. It lapped faster, its handling was more predictable, and it stopped better. Performance testing generated near-identical figures up to 130mph, though because of the Corvette's gearing the Nissan has a higher terminal speed. On the skidpad the Corvette achieved a production car best of 0.91g (300ZX: 0.88g). But the Nissan was nearly 5mph quicker through a 1,000ft slalom manoeuvrability test – and the fastest the magazine's test team had ever recorded. In normal road driving, however, they concluded that the 300ZX was streets ahead, and overall the Nissan won on points.

The verdict caused a storm of protest to descend on *Car and Driver* from devotees of America's home-grown champion sports car. Corvette fans were already smarting at the exclusion of the ZR-1 from the magazine's respected annual 'Ten Best' selection, nine of which were of Japanese origin (and included the 300ZX). Rivals *Motor Trend* avoid such controversy by choosing a domestic and an import car of the year; we have already noted that the 300ZX Turbo won the latter title for 1990.

But even the best cars have their failings. I have no reason to doubt the efficacy of the anti-lock braking system, but would like the pedal to be more communicative. Everyone agrees that the rear-quarter visibility is poor – a victim of styling – and I found that in some traffic conditions the steeply raked front pillars could also obscure the view.

The pods which concentrate controls either side of the steering wheel don't work quite as well as they look. They are nearly, but not quite, within finger-tip reach, but not very user-friendly even after long acquaintance. The rotary light switch is OK, but the matching wiper/washer control less convenient than a simple column stalk. The automatic climate control, the more elaborate of two air conditioning systems available, is fussy, noisy and too often blows cold air at you unnecessarily. It is standard in the UK market, but in the US comes with an

TESTED

Front seats are well-shaped and offer a wide range of adjustment, including, on driver's side, lumbar and side bolster support.

Rear seats of the 2+2 are more comfortable than many of the 'occasional' type. Right, main luggage well is shallow. In two-seater, an additional raised platform is provided between the suspension housings, which support the roller-blind cover.

Not for home mechanic! Bonnet of normally aspirated 300ZX, left, seems crowded until you compare it with the Turbo, right. Space was at such a premium that an extra-thin radiator and engine fan had to be devised.

electrically adjusted driver's seat and heated mirrors in the $900 Electronic Equipment Pack; this might be an option to avoid.

Similarly, not all buyers will think that leather-covered seats are worth an extra $1,000 (£1,150 in the UK, including the electric-adjust). They are the same Recaro-like shape, with lumbar and bolster adjustment, as those trimmed with the tasteful tweed cloth that forms the cockpit surrounds. These are good seats and most people can find a comfortable driving position in the 300ZX, though it would be easier for some if the steering column adjusted.

The two-seater cabin is the more pleasing aesthetically, but the way that the rear bulkhead is curved to wrap around each seat restricts backrest recline. The 'occasional' seats of the 2+2 are in themselves comfortable and supportive, but because leg- and head-room are limited, really only suitable for children. The passenger seat runs forward when the backrest is released to ease access to the rear but, in the infuriating Japanese way, the driver's seat backrest does not have a 'memory'.

To satisfy passive restraint regulations, US-market cars have their seat belts hung on the doors. 'Passive' protection is provided only if they are left buckled up so that opening the door provides a web of belts to slide under. Most 300ZX owners will regard belting-up as a routine part of driving and will use them as normal 'manual' belts, uncoupling the clasp at the centre (here labelled 'press in emergency') in the normal way. The US system has the incidental benefits of a more forward belt positioning and tidier stowage.

The 300ZX's luggage accommodation is not very generous. True, in the 2+2

TESTED

the load area can be extended by folding down the rear seat backs, but the two-seater's main luggage space only has room for one large suitcase. There is a smaller raised platform between the boxes that contain the spring/damper units (and stereo speakers) but that is not easy to get at from either the tailgate or the passenger doors. The option list in Japan includes a fitted oddments case for this space. Otherwise, stowage inside the cabin is restricted to a small drop-down glovebox and a shallow compartment below the centre armrest which is big enough for only a few cassettes or compact discs.

If the glass roof panels are removed, load space becomes even more of a problem. A vinyl pouch is provided to accommodate them and straps can secure them to the load area floor – provided, that is, that there is no luggage. Just as in earlier ZXs, the panels fit snugly and are easy to remove and replace at the flick of a lever. They are provided with black plastic shade panels which are OK when installed, but look cheap and damage-prone when lying around in the back.

Driving a 300ZX in the heat of the summer showed the value of those shades, for although the glass panels are screen-printed to provide some filtration, bright sun shining through the roof can be distracting. Travelling with the roof panels off isn't as nice as it might be, either. Nissan's extensive aerodynamic tests did not, it seems, include the effects of running topless, as the wind blows noisily and directly into the driver's ear...

Unlike some T-bar and Targa-topped cars, the 300ZX does not shake and rattle and this feeling of solidity and quality extends to the interior furnishings and the controls. Outside, one can criticize some of the plastic mouldings, especially the flimsy rear bumper cladding, the lower part of which has a crackle-finish to match the chip-resistant coating of the metal rocker panels.

Some colours suit the 300ZX's dramatic style much better than others. The US range of 11 shades includes the $350 option of pearl-glow white, blue or yellow. The latter, shown on the cover of this book, is particularly eye-catching, but absolutely unacceptable in Japan, where fashion has swung away from white, which dominated the cars of the 1980s, towards muted greys, blues and black. The first indications from UK dealers was that solid red was the most requested of five colours offered; that, incidentally, is the designers' choice as the most appropriate colour.

What is a 300ZX like to live with, month after month, year after year? The time of writing is too soon after launch to provide an index of reliability. *Car and Driver*'s experience in the first 20,000 miles of a long-term test of a Turbo has been joyous from a driving point-of-view, but also included a heater failure, clutch adjustment to cure what seemed like weak synchromesh on fourth gear, and premature replacement of front brake pads (at 18,000 miles). Other test cars were reluctant to produce full boost and suffered from uneven braking. In Britain, *Car*'s test of a pre-production UK-specification model reported inconsistent idling and weak synchromesh on fifth gear. These problems with hard-used test cars may not be typical; it is too early to know.

The widespread use of corrosion-resistant materials should allow the structure a longer life than its predecessors. Etching of the Vehicle Identification Number

A fast drive in the country

Nissan are well provided with test tracks. They have proving grounds with high-speed circuits at Tochigi, Murayama and Oppama, all within easy reach of Tokyo. There is a track in Arizona for hot-weather testing and a winter test facility is under construction on Hokkaido, Japan's northern island.

But, valuable as they are, most test tracks do not reproduce real road conditions very accurately. A key part of the development of the new 300ZX was the broadening of the experience of Nissan's test drivers. Apart from sharpening their technique at the Nurburgring racing school, they drove day in and day out on the German autobahns, sampled US highways – and also discovered the kind of country roads savoured by sports car owners on both sides of the Atlantic.

Japan is too crowded to offer many opportunities to extend a fast car on the open road. Armed with the knowledge from their travels, Nissan's development team suggested remodelling and extending the small 'country course' at the Tochigi Proving Ground.

What is now called the Marketability Evaluation Road runs through woodland. Many of the corners are blind; there are crests and dips, some fiendishly off-camber; the tarmac surface is smooth in parts, bumpy in others. Unlike most 'ride and handling' circuits, it is not a series of obviously artificial concrete hazards. In fact, it is just like a tricky European country road.

The 300ZX Turbo tackled its ups, downs, flicks and swerves with aplomb, even if after a couple of hot laps the air was acrid with the smoke of burning brake pads...

on all glass panels – standard on the US Turbo – should make the car somewhat less attractive to thieves; in some states that qualifies for an insurance discount.

The crowded engine compartment and the complexity of its electronics mean that the 300ZX is not an easy car for the home mechanic. Though the official service schedule is not unusually demanding (12,000 miles main interval, oil change at 6,000), any high-performance car demands extra care and attention to routine service items – fluid levels, tyre pressures and condition. With an average consumption of around 20 miles per Imperial gallon, the 300ZX Turbo does not have an unreasonable thirst for unleaded fuel.

Mindful of the 300ZX Turbo's potential, and the kind of company it keeps, the British importers have followed the practice of some other makers of exotic fast cars and made available to owners an introductory high performance driving course run by ex-Grand Prix driver Peter Gethin. It is a worthwhile extra, included in the price.

When all's said and done, there is still the question of image. By things you can measure, the 300ZX may better a 944 and be nearly half of the price of a comparable 928, but it still isn't a Porsche. Nissan know that you can't match a reputation built on 40 years of exclusive sports cars and the highest achievements in racing overnight and that the name on the back of the 300ZX may inhibit sales. But they are quietly confident that, longer term, attitudes will change. The new 300ZX has already begun that process.

PERFORMANCE

Model	300ZX n/a 2-seater	300ZX Turbo 2-seater	300ZX Turbo 2+2
Spec.	US	US	European
Source	— Car and Driver —		Car
Max. speed (mph)	143	153	155
0–30mph (sec)	2.2	2.0	2.1
0–40mph	3.5	3.1	3.0
0–50mph	4.9	4.2	4.4
0–60mph	6.7	5.5	5.7
0–70mph	9.0	7.2	7.7
0–80mph	11.3	9.3	9.7
0–90mph	14.2	11.6	11.9
0–100mph	18.6	14.6	15.2
0–110mph	23.6	18.0	18.7
0–120mph	30.2	22.6	23.6
0–130mph		30.9	—
Standing 1/4 mile	15.0	14.1	—
Top gear 50–70mph	10.1	8.5	—
Braking 70–0mph (ft)	171	169	—
Roadholding 300ft dia.(g)	0.86	0.88	—
Overall mpg (Imp)	20.4	18.0	19.6

Starting from Z

The generation gap – 20 years and 1.3 million cars separate the first 240Z and the latest 300ZX

In the the 1950s and 1960s, Britain ruled the sports car world. MGs, Triumphs and Austin-Healeys epitomized the affordable fun cars – open two-seaters with good performance and high style. The German and Italian marques were a higher order of things, in an exotic category with Jaguar, Aston Martin and others, which was out of reach to all but the rich.

The Datsun 240Z changed all that. It combined the shape of a Jaguar E-type and the size of a Porsche with the performance of the fastest Healey 3000 or Triumph TR, in a civilized coupe body. It looked terrific and at a starting price of less than $4,000 was an instant success on the US market.

It is a sad reflection on the state of the British motor industry at that time that they did nothing to respond to this strong new challenge from the East. They retreated, eventually to leave this section of the market altogether. Japan's Z-car was destined to become the best-selling sports car in history.

A quarter of a century ago the Japanese motor industry was not the high-tech, robotized model of efficiency that it is today. There were no Cray supercomputers, no sophisticated market research techniques. Nissan, like other Japanese car makers at the time, concentrated on small family cars, but they had already made a start with some sports cars that echoed the contemporary British two-seaters. They had started to sell the SP310 Fairlady 1500 in the United States. That car, which is sometimes erroneously described as an MGB copy (it was, in fact, revealed a year earlier than its British counterpart) was to develop into the SP311 1600 and the SR311 2000.

Factions within Nissan wanted to develop their sports car range beyond the upright open two-seater and to tailor something specifically for the US market. But their management remained unconvinced.

Albrecht Goertz, the German freelance designer who worked with Nissan's fledgling design studio in the early 1960s, recalls the casual way that the shape and style of the 240Z came about: 'I told them that, above all, the Americans wanted a two-seater with *room*.' Goertz had been at Porsche during the development of the 911 and favoured a fixed-head coupe rather than a traditional British roadster. Of existing cars, the 911 and the E-type Jaguar best represented their ambitions; the Porsche's size and the Jaguar's style. 'It was very unscientific, really. We simply said: "How long is a Porsche? How wide is a Jaguar?".'

The role that Goertz played in shaping the 240Z remains controversial. His was undoubtedly the inspiration for the kind of car that emerged, but by the time

Still on track – the 240Z was the fastest and best of the first series. The author covered 12,000 miles in this 1972 car, photographed here on the Spa-Francorchamps road circuit in Belgium.

Evolution – Nissan's first true sports car was the Fairlady Roadster, top. The German designer Albrecht Goertz, right, developed a coupe successor, centre, while working with Nissan in 1964. This can be seen as the starting point for the Z-car, but by an odd twist of fate emerged into the market as the Toyota 2000GT, below.

ORIGINS

it was launched in 1969 he was long gone. So, technically, had the prototype which he had designed.

By an odd twist of fate that car became, of all things, a Toyota. It happened like this: Nissan had sub-contracted development of their new sports car to Yamaha, whose facilities extend well beyond the motorcycles and musical instruments for which they are most famous. Goertz worked with Yamaha engineers on a project known as the 2000GT. When, towards the end of 1964, the completed car came to be reviewed by Nissan management, the 2-litre twin-cam engine that Yamaha had designed and built for it did not run properly. Nissan's bosses were not amused and the project was cancelled. Yamaha, as free agents, then approached Toyota with the idea of producing such a car; it became the expensive-to-build and short-lived Toyota 2000GT. A couple of years later, Nissan returned to the idea of a new sports/GT car and revived the Goertz design, hence the outward similarity between the Toyota 2000GT and the 240Z. As Goertz says: 'They could be brothers'.

The final car was different in many respects from his prototype, but the essential design elements remained: a lean-forward stance, the backward-sloping air intake, and a tight body/wheel relationship (with the wheels close to the outer extremities of the body and the tyre treads partly exposed as the wings cut away behind them).

Ten years later, after Goertz had commented unfavourably on the styling changes that created the 280ZX, Nissan denied that he had any involvement with the 240Z. Goertz was offended and sought to take legal action to protect his reputation. The matter was eventually settled out of court when Nissan sent him a letter which said: 'While it is our view that the design of the 240Z was the product of Nissan's design staff, Nissan agree that the personnel who designed that automobile were influenced by your fine work for Nissan and had the benefit of your designs.' Or, as Goertz puts it: 'They designed the car, but I showed them how'.

What everyone *did* agree back in 1969 when the 240Z was first presented was that here was a sensational car. It had the style of an exotic GT for the price of cheap sports car. There were better cars, for course, but none that offered what the Datsun did for the money. For the US retail starting price of $3,526, no-one else could offer a beefy overhead-camshaft six-cylinder engine, independent suspension all round, full creature comforts and the looks of an E-type. Not only that, but the 240Z promised the performance of a Porsche for the price of an MGB GT.

Peter Brock, who ran the highly successful BRE Datsun racing team on the US West Coast, remembers being shown some photographs of the 240Z in Japan some months before it was launched. 'At that time it was just the most beautiful car I'd ever seen. I said, "Is this a dream car?" and they said, "No, it's a production car for next year". Then they told me all the specifications and I went home on a cloud.'

The Datsun 240Z was aimed primarily at the US market and Nissan's local management recognized that racing would be important in establishing its credentials. The smartly turned-out BRE cars looked the part and started the Z's 10-year run of success in SCCA Production racing championhips.

Brock's team had been struggling with the Datsun 2000 Sports which, with its twin-cam four-cylinder engine was powerful enough but had such a narrow track that it was difficult to make it go round corners properly. The 240Z promised to change all that – and a racing programme was to play an important part in the way the new car was marketed in the United States.

The Sports Car Club of America was the heartland of the European sports car enthusiast, and their popular racing championships, conducted at regional level with end-of-season national finals, were important in establishing the right credentials for the Z-car.

This approach had backing at the highest level, for Yutaka Katayama, president of Nissan US, was a racing fan. 'Mr K', as he is affectionately known, had been a leading light in the establishment of the Sports Car Club of Japan. Nissan US supported two teams in SCCA racing at that time – Brock's BRE on the West Coast and Bob Sharp Racing in the East.

The Datsun 240Z won the SCCA C-Production National Championship two years in a row. By then, 40,000 Z-cars had been sold in the United States – and most dealers still held a waiting list. By 1972, annual sales in America were up to 50,000. This was a success beyond Nissan's hopes and expectations and required a rethink of production volumes, which had been set originally at 2,000 cars per month.

Manufacture of the Z had been sub-contracted to Nissan Shatai at Hiratsuka, an affiliate company that previously made the Fairlady roadsters and still builds the

ORIGINS

300ZX today. At its peak, Z-car production was to rise to 7,500 cars per month.

The 240Z confounded the industry's doubters, who said that it was becoming impossible to make any money out of making sports cars. Not only was it selling well but the Z-car was profitable. The volume helped of course – the MG plant at Abingdon was making less than 50,000 cars a year, and three different models, at that time – but the key was the relatively simple design utilizing mechanical components from other cars in the Nissan range. That was a trick learned from the British but, in a style that was to become familiar in the following years, the Japanese had applied it more effectively.

The 2.4-litre straight-six overhead-camshaft L24 engine was new, but closer examination shows that it was actually the L16 of the contemporary 510 Bluebird model with two more cylinders; pistons, connecting rods, bearings and valve gear were all shared with the saloon engine.

The standard four-speed gearbox of the original car was also derived from that of the 510, while the optional five-speed had already been developed for the 2000 Sports. The front suspension, using MacPherson struts with simple lower links and torque arms, was shared with the Laurel saloon. The strut-type rear suspension was unique to the 240Z, but one of the cheaper and simpler ways of achieving an independent rear end; there were marked similarities to Colin Chapman's layout for the original Lotus Elan.

According to the flattering SAE gross measurement of engine power (which is no longer used), the first 240Z produced 150bhp. Maximum speed was

The L24 straight-six engine of the 240Z was tough and powerful and served the marque well. Stretched to 2.8 litres and with fuel injection, it was used in all Z and ZX variants until the first 300ZX appeared in 1983. Contrast this underbonnet view of a pre-emission control Z with those of the new 300ZX on pages 74/75.

The Datsun team tried hard on the Monte Carlo Rally but their best finish was Rauno Aaltonen's third place in 1972. Tony Fall, shown here in the 1971 Monte, scored the Z's first European rally win, in the 1971 Welsh International.

The 240Z's greatest rally success was its two victories in the East African Safari. Rauno Aaltonen, left, was always a front-runner but didn't win; Shekhar Mehta, above right, was declared winner after a points tie in 1973.

125mph, it did 0–60mph in 8 seconds and was capable of a 16-second standing quarter-mile. These figures were better than the standard Porsche 911 or the Triumph TR6 and not far behind a 4.2-litre Jaguar E-type – though that had a much higher top speed.

So Datsun's new sports car could run with the best – and ahead of anything close to its US price. It handled well too, at least by the standards of the early 1970s. The hard low-speed ride was criticized, but comfort improved with speed and the senior British motoring magazine *Autocar* praised its 'very consistent handling characteristics'.

Just as the introduction in America had been linked with a racing programme, the European launch was accompanied by a sortie into international rallying. This gave the 240Z a somewhat inaccurate image as a big, hairy, brute of a car that filled the gap left by the heroic Austin-Healey 3000 on rallies, where a scientific revolution was dawning. By the standards of nimble, lightweight machines like the little Alpine-Renault, the rally Datsun *was* quite a handful, but the regular car was more inclined to understeer than oversteer unless intentionally provoked by too much throttle.

Of all motor sporting events, Nissan desperately wanted to win the East African Safari. They had been trying since 1963 and by 1969 the 1600 SSS (510) saloons had scored third place and taken the team prize. Ironically, at Easter 1970, as the 240Z was being tested in preparation for its Safari debut the following year, its saloon predecessor scored Nissan's greatest motor sport

ORIGINS

success. Edgar Herrmann, a German-born farmer from Malindi, Kenya, drove a Datsun to its first Safari success and was to have a repeat victory with a 240Z in 1971; a remarkable achievement for a car in its first full season of rallying on what was one of the longest and fastest Safaris.

The 240Z was to win the Safari again in 1973, when Shekhar Mehta squeezed home in a desperately battered car ahead of Datsun team-mate Harry Kallstrom.

The car never did as well in the classic European rallies. The best result was Rauno Aaltonen's third place in the 240Z's second attempt on the Monte Carlo Rally, in 1972, but there were outright wins in less prestigious events like the Welsh Rally and the Portuguese Rally of the Camelias. Further afield, Aaltonen was unlucky to lose the 1972 Southern Cross Rally in Australia because of an infringement of the rules about advertising on cars, and the same year a 240Z took second place in the Press-on-Regardless Rally, which was to be the US World Rally Championship qualifier.

All this activity helped the Datsun 240Z establish itself as the world's best-selling sports car. By 1973, the 240Z had comfortably out-distanced the British sports cars and the home-grown Chevrolet Corvette. But increasingly stringent exhaust emissions regulations were beginning to take their toll on the car's performance and driveability. Its weight had increased because of the additional emissions control equipment and the need for strengthened and extended bumpers to meet insurance-dictated Federal rules. An increase in engine displacement was the only way to cope with these new demands, and in 1964 the 240Z became the 260Z.

With the 2.6-litre engine came an alternative 2+2 body style, 12 inches longer than the two-seater but with the front-end styling as the original. Though, to some extent, it redressed the performance loss of the restricted US-spec cars, British tests showed that the 260Z was heavier and slower to accelerate than the first 240Z. But the 2+2 widened the model's market; in retrospect, its arrival can be seen as the start of the Z-car's evolution from pure sports car towards luxury GT.

The Z's launch on to the British market had been well behind the introductions in the US and Japan. A 240Z was shown at the London Motor Show in October 1970, but Datsun UK were not then sure if they would import the model. When they decided to do so, supplies were slow in arriving; the first cars did not get to customers until the summer of 1971. It was much less of a bargain than in the USA and in the UK it found itself competing in the market with cars like the Alfa Romeo 1750GTV, Lotus Elan, and Porsche 914; the 240Z price of £2,288 compared with £1,356 for an MGB GT. It was not surprising, then, that sales were relatively low and that customers were likely to be older, and wealthier, than in the US. This clientele favoured the 2+2 version and from 1976 the 260Z two-seater virtually disappeared from the European market.

In America, the 260Z didn't last for long as the ever-tightening emissions regulations had made the carburettor engine temperamental – difficult to start and prone to hesitation and surging. For 1975, the switch was made to fuel

300ZX

The 240Z became the 2.6-litre 260Z, left, in 1973. At the same time, the Z range was broadened with the introduction of the longer-wheelbase 2+2, below, which lost the two-seater's purity of line.

ORIGINS

Emissions and safety legislation in the United States brought the fuel-injected 2.8-litre 280Z with its elongated bumpers in 1975, right. This version was not sold in Europe.

injection and, at the same time the displacement was 'stretched' to 2.8 litres. The 280Z brought an immediate improvement in driveability and also better performance – though it still didn't match the first 240Zs, which were unfettered by safety and emissions control equipment. That was not surprising really, for the the 280Z weighed nearly 5cwt more than the original. It was heavier to drive as well, what with the extra weight and wider tyres, so that power steering began to be demanded – though it was never made available.

The 280Z was never sold in Europe, but took Z-car sales in America to a new high – 70,000 cars in 1977. It was clear that the US market was changing, or perhaps that the development of the Z itself had changed the market. Even if it was no faster than its predecessors, the 280Z was better equipped and more refined. Automatic transmission had become a popular option. The price had risen steadily and Mazda had launched the Wankel-engined RX7 beneath it, aimed at the customers who had eagerly purchased the 240Z eight years earlier. Nissan decided not to compete with the Mazda, but to move the Z-car further up-market. Hence the 280ZX.

Whereas the 240Z was an intuitive car, created in Japan with input from Albrecht Goertz and others, the 280ZX was a product of market research, particularly in America. The manager of the Product Development Group at Nissan US was an Englishman, Peter Harris, who is now a key member of the management team for Nissan's Infiniti luxury car programme. He explains the thinking behind the 280ZX when it was launched in November 1978: 'We felt we were out of the market for a purist sports car. For the new car we wanted performance and handling, but with a lot of comfort, power windows, cruise control and so on: a US 'personal' car. We got what we wanted.'

The sales pitch for the ZX was directed away from those who bought and loved the Z and towards those who had been shocked by energy crises to 'downsize' from Cadillacs and Thunderbirds. 'Luxury in the Fast Lane' became its slogan.

To make the new car bigger, heavier and more elaborate than its predecessor was against the trends of the time, when the emphasis was on fuel economy. It certainly did not please the true sports car enthusiast. But it worked – in 1979 US sales were higher than ever before.

There was nothing bad about the 280ZX, it was simply different. Not very different in the way it looked – the long nose with the 'sugar scoop' headlamp surrounds ensured visual continuity – but enough to seem fat and flabby. It was expressing this to *Car and Driver* that got Albrecht Goertz into trouble with Nissan, but many shared his disappointment that the new car had lost the Z's lithe, rarin'-to-go appearance.

Two-seater and 2+2 versions of the 280ZX were designed in parallel, and of the two the longer 2+2 has the better-balanced shape. Whatever one's view of the styling, these were more scientifically designed than their predecessors. The ZX was the first Nissan to be thoroughly tested in the wind-tunnel at the design stage, and although a drag coefficient of 0.385 does not seem very impressive today, it was a major improvement on the 0.467 Cd of the first Z.

The ZX was not, as some thought at the time of its introduction, an elaborate 'facelift' of the 280Z. It was a new car from the ground up, with only the fuel-injected 2.8-litre engine and the transmission carried over from the old model. A major change was to the rear suspension, which abandoned the strut system for a semi-trailing-arm set-up, shared with the contemporary Nissan 810 saloon. MacPherson struts continued at the front, though with tension rods running forward instead of trailing as on the Z.

Power steering became an essential option, while the disc/drum braking system of the Z was supplanted by disc brakes all round, with ventilated rotors at the front. Though capable of surprisingly high cornering speeds, the 280ZX proved less agile than the Z. Its performance against the stopwatch was also less impressive; in a 1980 test, *Autocar* recorded a maximum speed of only 112mph for a 280ZX two-seater, which struggled to break 10 seconds for 0–60mph acceleration.

But the 280ZX was quiet, relatively refined, and loaded with goodies, especially when fitted out with the US Grand Luxury package, as many were. It was perfect for its intended market.

The first major revision for the ZX was the T-bar roof. Nissan have never entertained the idea of a full convertible Z-car, but twin removable roof panels were gaining favour with American manufacturers as a way of providing open-air motoring without having completely to redesign the body structure. The smoked glass panels for the 280ZX fit well and are easy to remove or lock into

By 1978, the demand for more space and more equipment had produced a new series of Z-cars, the 280ZX. Once again, two-seater, below, and 2+2 versions were offered, though with a better balance between the styles. The T-bar roof became a popular option from the 1980 model year.

place. By the end of 1980, its first year on the options list, more than 50% of US sales were T-bar versions.

By 1981, with fuel crises receding into memory, Nissan judged that the time was right to introduce a more powerful version to the US market. A turbocharged engine developing 180bhp (35 more than the standard 280ZX of the time) was made available for the T-roof two-seater, at first only with automatic transmission. Uprating the power unit brought with it an improved, rack-and-pinion power steering system, changes in suspension settings and bigger wheels and tyres.

Here, at last, was a Z-car that was faster than the original 240Z! Even with automatic transmission, it pleased enthusiasts. *Road & Track*, who found it did

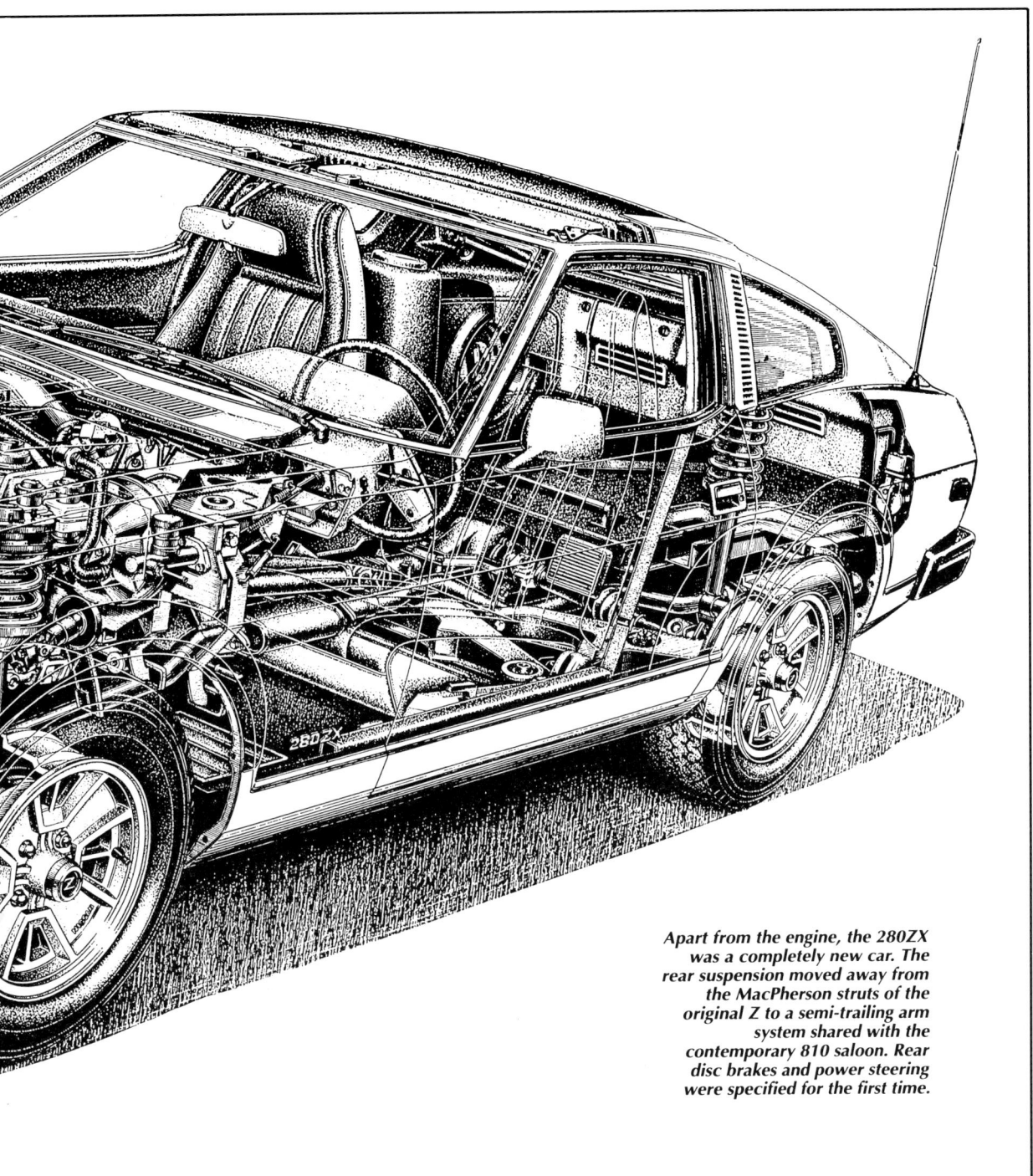

Apart from the engine, the 280ZX was a completely new car. The rear suspension moved away from the MacPherson struts of the original Z to a semi-trailing arm system shared with the contemporary 810 saloon. Rear disc brakes and power steering were specified for the first time.

300ZX

'Luxury in the fast lane' was the way that the 280ZX was presented in America. Even the two-seater, left, had become less of a sports car and more of boulevard cruiser. Dynamically, the 280ZX wasn't bad, below, but by 1980 others were doing better.

ORIGINS

In America, Nissan celebrated the Z-car's 10th birthday in 1980 with this garish black-and-gold anniversary edition 280ZX.

The 280ZX Turbo was described as a '1981½' model and signalled the Z-car's return to high performance.

The VG30 3-litre V6 took the place of the faithful straight-six engine in the 300ZX. Though much of the structure remained as before, the Z31 body was new and much improved aerodynamically, thanks to extensive wind tunnel work, below.

ORIGINS

129mph and 0–60mph in 7.4 seconds, called it 'one of the most exciting and satisfying cars we have driven in years'. For 1982 a 2+2 Turbo became available and so did a five-speed manual gearbox version. Though some were sold in left-hand drive European markets, the 280ZX Turbo was never offered in Britain. Nor, indeed, was it available in the Japanese domestic market, where the 280ZX was known, like its predecessors, as the Fairlady Z.

In Japan, for taxation reasons, Nissan continued to sell Z-cars with a 2-litre straight-six engine. But in world markets the ZX six-cylinder was beginning to show its age, and with the 280ZX Turbo it had reached the limit of its development. Mindful not only of the ZX, but also of future requirements for saloon cars, Nissan developed a new 3-litre V6. The VG30 engine was designed to be versatile, durable and easy to maintain. So it had to be compact and strong and include such features as self-adjusting hydraulic tappets.

This new engine, producing 170bhp in normally-aspirated form and 228bhp with a turbocharger, made its debut in the ZX in September 1983. Again, enthusiasts for the early Zs were disappointed that Nissan had not taken advantage of the reduced size and weight of the new engine to produce a smaller and handier car but we now know that was in mind for the future – and the result forms the main subject of this book. In the interim was another 300ZX, which was, literally, a facelifted 280ZX equipped with the new engine. It wasn't lighter – in fact, it was substantially heavier overall – but in 1984 it could claim to be the fastest-ever Japanese production car.

US Turbo versions, with 205bhp, had a maximum speed of about 135mph and 0–60mph acceleration in 7.3 seconds, while the corresponding figures for a British-market car without catalytic convertor and other US emissions gear were 140mph and 7.0 seconds. This performance, like the UK price, ventured into Porsche 944 territory for the first time.

Though the floorpan and essential dimensions remained the same as for the

Z-car, 1987-style – Nissan's San Diego studio tidied-up the 300ZX with new integrated bumpers, extended wheelarches and rocker panels, all in body colour.

Historical setting – 1972 Datsun 240Z and 1985 Nissan 300ZX Turbo 2+2, earliest and last ancestors of the new 300ZX.

280ZX, the outer body panels were all new and Nissan claimed (though not everyone believed) that the drag coefficient had come down to 0.30. The most striking feature was the more drooping nose section, allowed by the shorter engine, and incorporating distinctive semi-retractable headlamps.

Two-seater and 2+2 versions were cleverly styled to be hard to distinguish at a glance; only the extended rear quarter-window gives an outward clue. Most cars were supplied with the glass-panelled T-roof which, combined with a black lateral rubbing strip and spoilers, and the Turbo's bonnet-top air intake, gave the basically clean shape an 'add-on' look.

Later versions were tidied-up by rounding the nose section and using body colour for bumpers and appendages. They also wore the flared wheelarches and sill extensions that were first seen on a special edition that celebrated the 50th anniversary of the Nissan Motor Company in 1984.

At the time of the first 300ZX launch, *Autocar*'s Japanese correspondent concluded that it had 'the power but not the manners of a supercar'. That serves as a good summary for the fuller reports that later appeared on both sides of the Atlantic. The new model brought further development of the suspension, which included the option of cockpit-adjustable shock absorbers.

These changes brought more precise handling and better steering response, though at some penalty in ride comfort, even when taking advantage of the three alternative damper settings. The chassis is competent, but does not have the balance of a Porsche 944 nor the comfortable compromise between ride and handling of a GT car like a Jaguar XJ-S.

State-of-the-art technology offered for the 300ZX included electronic anti-lock braking and a four-speed automatic transmission with lock-up devices and electronic control, providing two automatically-selected shift programmes. Some of the interior equipment available smacked of gimmickry – power seat controls providing eight-way adjustments, a tilt steering column with a memory, and an electronic facia display.

As it turned out, the most significant version of the first 300ZX was restricted to the home market. In 1986 Japanese customers, who are always impressed by technology, were able to buy a Fairlady 300ZR with a four-camshaft, four-valves-per-cylinder version of the VG30 engine. Just as the V6 had shown Nissan's thoughts for the future – it is now used, mounted transversely and driving the front wheels of the Maxima saloon as well as in other domestic models – so, the 24-valve VG30DE gave a sign. The next Z-car would have a more sophisticated engine, which would make the ZX chassis look old-fashioned by comparison.

Ideally, a completely new car was needed. The bigger, faster, fancier, market-led progression that had developed the 240Z into the 300ZX had run its course. It was time to go back to a real sports car, to revive the spirit of the 240Z, 20 years on.

Enter the new 300ZX...

ORIGINS

Close relations – Nissan 200SX, right, also sold as the 240SX in the US and the 180SX/Silvia in Japan, was designed by same group as the 300ZX and uses the same multi-link rear suspension. Second generation Mid-4 prototype from 1987, centre, had much of the new ZX's engine and suspension technology, but its four-wheel drive was not adopted for the 300ZX. Instead, the Skyline GT-R, bottom, became Nissan's 4WD performance car. It also has multi-link suspension front and rear and Super HICAS.

A racing certainty

From the earliest days, Nissan have kept on track with the Z-car. Today, the 300ZX is only part of an ambitious racing programme

Racing was an essential part of the US marketing programme for the original 240Z. It helped the Z gain its credentials as a genuine sports car and, in a broader sense, to establish Nissan – or, rather, Datsun at that time – as makers of something more than boring econo-boxes.

The Z-car was to enjoy a remarkable run of success in SCCA events. John Morton started a decade's domination of the C-Production category by winning the national championship in 1970 and 1971 for Pete Brock's BRE team. This Nissan-supported operation on the West Coast was matched by Bob Sharp Racing in Connecticut. Bob Sharp had won Datsun's first SCCA Championship title driving a 1600 Roadster in 1967 and was to go on to three C-Production titles in Zs.

Sharp's first 240Z became the most successful of them all. An early show vehicle that was released to the competitions department after an over-enthusiastic (or perhaps just over-weight) photographic model dented its roof, it passed from Sharp to Jim Fitzgerald, and between them it raced for 10 years, started over 120 races, and 'won too often to count'. Like any well-used race car, it was about as original as George Washington's axe by the end, and like most early Zs on the tracks it eventually became a 280Z.

By 1980 it was estimated that there were as many as 250 Z-cars active in amateur racing in the USA and Nissan could claim to have the largest competition parts operation in the world. Though the roadgoing Z was turning progressively from sports car to luxury GT, Nissan kept up the pressure on the circuits and in its first year the 280ZX was an SCCA Champion. The record books show the driver as P.L.Newman.

The world knows 'PLN' as Paul Newman, superstar. He had become interested in racing when making the film *Winning* and had taken to SCCA Production events, scoring his first National Championship in 1976 driving a Triumph TR6. He subsequently drove in Bob Sharp's Datsun team and in 1979, armed with a new 280ZX, won six out of eight races to become North East Divisional Champion and then beat the similar cars of Logan Blackburn and Bob Leitzinger in the SCCA National Championship run-offs at Road Atlanta.

Newman is quite a guy. He clearly enjoys being part of the racing fraternity and, as far as anyone can who is a household name all over the world, stops being a film star and becomes just another competitor at race weekends. There he allows no hordes of hangers-on or show-biz interviews. The racing people

ON TRACK

P.L. Newman – Nissan racing driver.

like him for that – and respect him as a driver who can still win races in his 60s and as a patron of some pretty heavyweight professional teams.

PLN was the driver of the machine that moved Nissan in the USA from Production racing with basically standard cars towards the altogether more serious business of purpose-built race cars. As well as SCCA racing, they were well represented in the increasingly important series run in the USA by the International Motor Sports Association (IMSA). Their specialist in this category was the Electramotive team from El Segundo, California, run by John Knepp and Don Devendorf; Devendorf won the IMSA GTU Championship in 1979 driving a 2.5-litre 280ZX. Bob Sharp Racing were in there too, with Sam Posey scoring a couple of notable successes, but the GTU rules favoured the rotary-powered Mazda RX7s and Nissan began to look to higher things. 'We didn't like playing second fiddle at IMSA races', Bob Sharp recalls. 'We wanted to run with the big cars.' Hence the project to build a Porsche 935 challenger – a 700bhp ZX for Paul Newman to drive in IMSA's premier class.

IMSA rules required them to use an engine of the same make as the original car. Sharp obtained a 4.5-litre pushrod V8 engine from a Nissan President limousine, fitted it with Lucas fuel injection and a pair of turbochargers, and commissioned CanAm racing specialist Trevor Harris to produce a multi-tube chassis frame which could be grafted to a 280ZX centre section and clothed with a lightweight body that was a loose facsimile of the road car.

Only the shape's the same – the latest IMSA GTO 300ZX race car.

The ZX V8 Turbo ran for the first time in 1980 and raced throughout 1981, but was never a great success. IMSA admitted pure prototypes, Lola and March

300ZX

The most successful racing Z-car, left, started out as Bob Sharp's first 240Z, evolved into a 280Z, and was still winning races 10 years later in the hands of Nissan stalwart Jim Fitzgerald. Bob Sharp Racing have continued to be an official Nissan team ever since. Their first 280ZX racer, below, was driven by Paul Newman.

ON TRACK

sports-racers, into what was then the GTX class and the heavy front-engined Nissan was outclassed. It did, however, lead the way to the Electramotive team's first IMSA GTP prototype built on a Lola chassis in 1984 – and to its successors that dominated this class of racing at the end of the decade.

Meanwhile, Don Devendorf had moved into the IMSA GTO class with a production-derived 280ZX Turbo and won the 1982 GTO Championship. Sharp and Newman moved back to SCCA racing, with cars for both the amateur GT-1 and the professional TransAm classes. For 1984 these became 300ZXs, with 2.8 litre V6 engines installed in tube-frame chassis, and though Newman had a disappointing time in TransAm, veteran team-mate Jim Fitzgerald did win the national GT-1 championship. But The Hustler was back in 1985 and 1986, winning the amateur title twice in a row. A year later the GT-1 laurels went to Scott Sharp, son of the team's founder, in a 300ZX.

Towards the end of the 1970s, Showroom Stock racing – allowing only safety modifications plus a change of brake pads, shock absorbers and engine 'blueprinting' – gained in importance in the US. 280Zs were early winners and their success continued in the mid-1980s with the first 300ZX Turbo. Scott Sharp and Pepe Pombo dominated the 1988 SCCA Escort Endurance Championship.

For 1989, the arrival of the new 300ZX provided a fresh opportunity. The Nissan prototype, driven by Geoff Brabham, had steamrollered through the 1988 Camel GTP Championship. The new 240SX was the ideal basis for a contender in the GTU class (and sure enough, Bob Leitzinger's SX was to beat the Mazdas to win the championship). What the Japanese needed was a winner in the GTO category, where silhouette replicas of Detroit compacts and threatening interlopers like Audi Quattros had been looking good.

While the new road car was being readied for launch, the Nissan US competitions department was working secretly on a racing version. It would not, in truth, bear any more than a superficial relationship with the 300ZX that was arriving at the showrooms. IMSA rules require GTO cars to share only engine position and configuration with the original, plus a few key body components, like the A-posts and the roof. They are supposed to look like the real thing, but most of them don't; the sensible manufacturer makes sure that the car's identity is writ large along with the sponsors on the sides.

Though controlled more directly by Nissan than its predecessors, the development of the GTO 300ZX was entrusted to the same Electramotive team that had been so successful with the GTP racer, notably John Knepp, Don Devendorf, Wes Moss and Trevor Harris. Harris drew up a complex tubular spaceframe chassis which would not look out of place for a Maserati 'Birdcage' restoration. Much of its equipment is straight from the GTP prototype, including the engine, which though it can claim an inheritance from the VG30 V6, is actually quite different from that which powers the latest 300ZX.

The IMSA engine has an aluminium block, specially cast in America for Electramotive, but the cylinder heads have single cams and only two valves per

cylinder. The GTP version is 3 litres, but the rules allow it only one turbocharger; for GTO the capacity is reduced to 2.75 litres, but twin turbos can be fitted (because the road car is so equipped). Much of the success of this engine is put down to the management system developed by electronics wizard Don Devendorf, who has been able to optimize it every time new regulations have been introduced to even out the GTP cars' performance. Specific restrictions in each class mean that the power output of both GTP and GTO versions is similar, at 690bhp.

In their first season, the two 300ZX GTO cars, run by Cunningham Racing and driven by Steve Millen and John Morton, were found to be in need of further development. Millen won at the fast Road America circuit at Elkhart Lake, Wisconsin, but turbo lag was a disadvantage on twistier circuits and the drivers found them quite a handful. 1990 started better, for at the opening IMSA round at Miami, Nissan won all three classes – GTP, GTO and GTU. Among a variety of modifications for the new season, the 1990 car has a longer wheelbase and Number 1 driver Steve Millen reported that it is 'quicker, easier to drive, and easier to set-up'.

The 1989 season did, however, confirm officially what everyone in racing knew – that Nissan were the undisputed champions in IMSA GTP. Though Geoff Brabham had won an unprecedented eight races in a row in 1988, Nissan had lost the manufacturers' championship to Porsche by one point. The following year 10 wins out of 15 starts made sure of the title, the first for a Japanese manufacturer in IMSA's premier series.

The mighty IMSA ZX Turbo was a front-engined prototype powered by a Nissan President V8. It was not a great success, the development being overtaken by the arrival in IMSA of pure mid-engined sports-racers.

ON TRACK

In October 1989, Nissan took over the Electramotive operation and re-established it as Nissan Performance Technology Inc in Vista, California, responsible for all their performance vehicle development, design and construction in the USA. Don Devendorf, though still a senior scientist at the Hughes aircraft company, became president of the new organization.

In recent years Nissan's racing efforts have extended from North America to a full-scale attack on the World Sports Car Championship, the domain of Porsche, Jaguar and Mercedes-Benz. When it started in 1986, this British-based programme used a March Group C chassis with an early Electramotive IMSA V6 engine – standard cast-iron block – developed with twin turbochargers to produce 700bhp in race trim and up to 1,000bhp for short periods in qualifying.

In 1987 the V6 was supplanted by the VRH30 V8 – a four-cam, 32-valve twin-turbo race engine specially designed in Japan. For 1989, that became the 3.5-litre VRH35, with output quoted as 'over 800bhp'. Lola Cars provided the state-of-the-art R89C composite chassis. The Group C effort was centralized under a newly-formed subsidiary, Nissan Motorsports Europe Ltd, based in Milton Keynes, England, with Howard Marsden as resident director. As this is written, it has yet to achieve better than third place in a WSC round, but the team is improving all the time.

In Tokyo, the president of Nissan Motorsports International (NISMO) is Yasuharu Nanba, a man who has long been associated with the Z-car story. In the early 1970s he had been the manager of the part of the Vehicle Test Department which was responsible for the 240Z rally programme. In 1984, at

The original 300ZX, prepared by Bob Sharp Racing and driven by Paul Newman, below, Jim Fitzgerald and Scott Sharp, took a series of SCCA GT-1 titles. Its successor, shown overleaf, made its debut in the IMSA GTO series in 1989 driven by Steve Millen and John Morton. Morton drove the successful BRE 240Zs back in 1970s.

300ZX

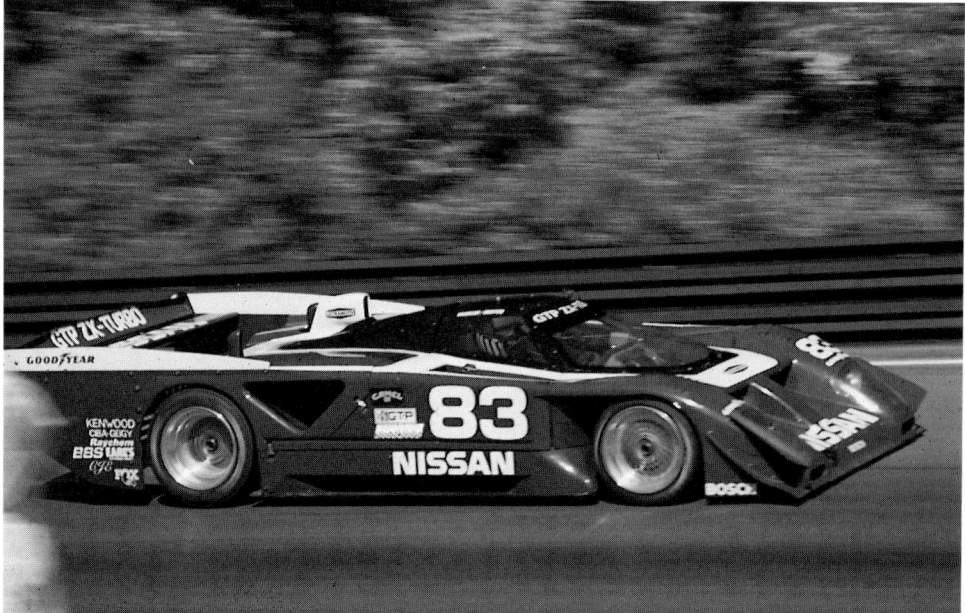

For more than two seasons there has been nothing to touch the Nissan ZX prototype in IMSA GTP racing. The Electramotive car driven by Geoff Brabham, son of three times world champion Sir Jack, has been the regular winner, as here at Mid-Ohio in 1988.

ON TRACK

The R89 Group C car is superficially similar to the IMSA GTP machine but has V8 rather than V6 power. Latest R90CK is a development of 1989 car.

Don Devendorf.

the very start of the research into the all-new 300ZX, he was briefly its project leader before going back to take charge of the company's racing and rallying activities worldwide.

Motor sport has changed since the days when a car like the 240Z could give a good account of itself in professional racing and rallying and be used by amateurs for everything from sprints to autocross. Nissan's strategy today is to use different cars for different events – the IMSA and Group C prototypes for top-class racing; the 300ZX and 200SX for production-based events in the USA; the Skyline GT-R for saloon car racing, notably in Japan and Australia; and a new small four-wheel-drive saloon for international rallying from 1991.

What of the future? How far will Nissan go to prove their worth in competition against the world's best? According to president Yutaka Kume, speaking at the Tokyo Motor Show in 1989, they could go all the way to the top: 'Experience is what counts in racing and we are accumulating experience in Group C and other events. At the moment that has all our resources, but ultimately, some day in the future, we would like to tackle Formula 1'.

300ZX